CW00547939

Liqu

Liquid Church

Pete Ward

WIPF & STOCK · Eugene, Oregon

Wipf and Stock Publishers
199 W 8th Ave, Suite 3
Eugene, OR 97401

Liquid Church
By Ward, Peter
Copyright©2002 by Ward, Peter
ISBN 13: 978-1-62032-980-1
Publication date 3/15/2013
Previously published by Hendrickson, 2002

To

Andrew Walker

CONTENTS

Preface   ix

Introduction   1

Part One: Solid Church

1. Solid and Liquid Modernity and the Church   13

2. The Mutations of Solid Church: Heritage, Refuge,   22
    and Nostalgia

Part Two: Liquid Church

3. Liquid in Christ   33

4. Network and Flow in the Liquid Church   40

5. The Liquid Dance of God   49

6. Shaping the Liquid Church   56

7. Regulating the Flow, Part One: The Word of God   65

8. Desire for God   72

9. Regulating the Flow, Part Two: The Spirit and Grace   78

10. Inside the Liquid Church   87

Notes   99

Bibliography   109

PREFACE

A chance observation led to the writing of this book: in a discussion with Jonny Baker I started to reflect on the success and failure of contemporary forms of church. In a variety of places and in conversation with different groups of people I have been able to develop these thoughts. My thanks go to Greenbelt Festival, The British and Irish Association for Mission Studies, Cultural Shift, and The Centre for Youth Ministry in Cambridge. All have entertained versions of liquid church. I am grateful for the opportunity to sharpen my ideas through debate. At King's College, London, I am fortunate to be part of a growing community of researchers working on issues of gospel, culture, and mission. Under the watchful eyes of Andrew Walker and Steve Holmes I have been able to test my ideas. I am increasingly excited by my membership in these groups and for the stimulation and enthusiasm to create and write that they bring.

Along the way I have given sections of the book to various friends and colleagues for their comment and critique. I am particularly in the debt of Chris Russell, Steve Griffiths, and Simon Hall for their helpful comments. I have mostly ignored what they have said, but I suspect they didn't imagine that I would do anything other than this. Finally I want to say a huge thank you to my colleague and mentor Professor Andrew Walker. This book would probably have remained an interesting and provocative paper given at a few conferences if it had not been for Andrew's enthusiasm to try and find a publisher for it. For this and for all the other kindnesses while we have worked together at Kings College, London, I thank him.

Pete Ward

INTRODUCTION

The church of God must not stand still. In every age, inspired by the Holy Spirit, God's people have found new ways to express their fellowship and mission. As Philip Hefner puts it, "the church is never static and cannot make permanent the forms that prove effective in any particular time and place."[1] The challenges raised by evolving cultures and the events of history have always been met by innovation in church life. This fact was expressed by the Reformers' use of the phrase *"Ecclesia semper reformanda est"*—the church is continually in need of renewal.[2] Change is basic to the nature of the church, but not all change is good or right. Some changes leave the church marginalized in society and dislocated from its calling. *Liquid Church* argues that such changes in the wider culture have adversely affected the communal life and witness of the church, which means that church as we know it has a number of problems. Not least of these problems is the church's ability to be an effective agent for mission in the culture. We need a new reformation to renew and refresh our church if it is to be faithful to its purpose and its Lord.

HEALTH WARNING

At the start I want to give a health warning: liquid church does not exist yet. Moreover, please do not think that I have set up and run a successful, thriving liquid church. This means that what I say here is an attempt to imagine rather than describe a different way of being church. So this book is not a prepackaged how-to manual for contemporary ministry. However, I feel that some people in the UK and the US are looking for a vision of a new way of being God's people in worship and mission. In response I have tried to develop such a vision, so at its heart this book is an act of theological imagination.

What Is Liquid Church?

To get the imaginative juices flowing I suggest that we need to shift from seeing church as a gathering of people meeting in one place at one time—that is, a congregation—to a notion of church as a series of relationships and communications. This image implies something like a network or a web rather than an assembly of people. An example of this was given to me by a research student who saw nothing strange in the idea of a liquid church made up of informal relationships instead of formal meetings. He explained that before we met for our academic seminar, he was in a coffee shop with one of his Christian friends. As they talked, he said, he felt that Christ was communicated between them. For him this was church. This is the familiar notion of fellowship, but when one adds the definite article to the word *fellowship,* it takes on a different character. "The fellowship" indicates a more structured, static, and formal notion of church. My phrase for describing this shift toward structures, institutions, and meetings is solid church.

So the first move in imagining a liquid church is to take the informal fellowship, in which we experience Christ as we share with other Christians, and say this is church. Maybe this idea is neither threatening nor revolutionary. However, the implications are profound. First, it implies that church might be something that we make with each other by communicating Christ, so it is not an institution as such. Second, it indicates that church happens when people are motivated to communicate with each other. In other words, its basis lies in people's spiritual activity rather than in organizational patterns or buildings. Third and more controversially, I suggest that a liquid church does not need or require a weekly congregational meeting. In place of going to church, the emphasis could be on living as Christ's body in the world. Worship and meeting with others will still have a place, but worship and meeting will be decentered and reworked in ways that are designed to connect to the growing spiritual hunger in society rather than being a place for the committed to belong (i.e., some kind of religious club).

This description raises the question of social organization. What will liquid church look like? My response is to point to the way in which contemporary media, business, and finance are based on networks of communication. The argument is that communication of Christ through informal fellowship creates connections, groupings, and relationships. These can be seen as a kind of network where the Holy Spirit is at work creating church. Stuart Murray described this to me as the shift from church as a noun to church as a verb. So we can say, "I church, you church, we church." For too long we have seen church as something that we attend. We might sing a few hymns or even play a more active role, but there is something passive and even a little alienating about the externalized and rather monolithic idea of church. If, however, church is something that comes about when we make it, then walls come tumbling down. Suddenly being church and doing church become an exciting adventure.

The next move in this imaginatory exercise is to ask what is the place of the various productive and creative processes that characterize contemporary Christian culture. By this I mean festivals, worship music, evangelism courses, and other processes. At present the institution of the church, local or national, seems to be largely irrelevant to these creative and productive activities. The whole web of entrepreneurial activity and dynamism that makes much of our evangelism and worship effective (and fun) is sort of, but not really, church. Liquid church would address this issue by saying that as these individuals, organizations, and groups carry out their activities, they are being or doing church. Moreover, as we participate in and use these groups' events and products, we are also being or making church. It is provocative to use the language of consuming and commodities, but it is deliberate, because it points toward my main motivation for suggesting why we need a new pattern in church life: mission.

Liquid church is essential because existing patterns of church fail to connect with the evident spiritual interest and hunger that we see in the UK and the US. For some people, church as we know it is rewarding. Sunday worship is a meaningful activity, and the fellowship is a place where we can serve Christ and establish our identity with other Christians. For these people and for those who lead their congregations, liquid church is not a matter of urgency. I understand this, and I am sympathetic to the successful church. It lacks credibility to claim that these large churches will wither and die in the face of cultural change (whatever term we use for it—

post-Christian, post-Christendom, postmodern). The problem is not with those who come to church, since it seems for
them church is generally a positive environment. The real
issue must be those who no longer attend church or those who
have never set foot inside one. How do we connect with these
people? Linked to this is the growing feeling among some
young adults and young people that church needs to be different to connect with their cultural sensibilities. Many of these
people are starting to experiment with new patterns of church
life. It is my conviction that the theological imagination used
in this book to describe a church based on dynamic, informal
relationships and the producing and consuming of events and
products will help these emerging churches. At the same time
it should help those interested in mission and evangelism to
overcome some of the problems they experience in sharing
the faith in contemporary culture. Both of these groups need a
new kind of church.

Finally, as part of this health warning I should add that I
use the language of Reformation (as opposed to revolution)
deliberately. In the sixteenth century, church life changed in
radical ways, but the Catholic Church did not melt away;
rather, it also reformed itself. My dream for this vision of liquid
church is that we will see similar things happening. Some
people will set out on a new and radical course. Others will adjust what they are doing. Both reactions to this vision are fine.
We need more variety in church life. There's little point in replacing one monochrome culture with another.

DESCRIBING CHURCH SOCIOLOGICALLY AND THEOLOGICALLY

Descriptions of church are problematic. Paul Tillich makes
a distinction between "sociological" and "theological" discus-
sions of church, pointing out that the church is something of a
paradox. On the one hand it exists in the "ambiguities of life in
general," while on the other hand it is connected to what
he calls "the unambiguous life of the Spiritual Community."[3]
These two aspects, the theological and sociological, will be
used together as I argue for a new, liquid approach to church.
The sociological discussion within *Liquid Church* relates to
changes in the economic and social experience of modernity.
Chapter 1 describes modernity as dividing into two phases,
solid and liquid modernity, both of which have affected the

church. I argue that patterns of church life have evolved so that church has developed to imitate some of the solid features of contemporary life. I call this solid church. In the liquid phase of modernity, this solid church has mutated into three forms: heritage, refuge, and nostalgic communities. These changes are described in chapter 2 in terms of personal identity and community in the new, fluid culture of modernity. The downside of changes in the solid church is that its various mutations render it limited in its ability to reach out to significant numbers of people in the fluidity of contemporary culture.

Chapter 3 starts the theological exploration of a liquid church by introducing Paul's theology of participation "in Christ." The apostle's corporate Christology becomes a starting point for a new ecclesiology. At the heart of this discussion is the possibility of a more fluid understanding of unity and diversity in the body of Christ. Chapter 4 introduces the idea of the network as the primary social structure in liquid church. Sociological descriptions of contemporary economic life as flows of communication through complex networks indicate a way forward for the church. Chapter 5 returns to the theological basis for liquid church by linking the idea of flows of relationship to recent discussion of the doctrine of the Trinity. The intimate communication and *perichoresis,* or mutual indwelling, of Father, Son, and Holy Spirit is expressed as a flowing movement or dance. This dance opens up for our participation as we join in with the mission and worship of God who is three and one.

I argue that we can see aspects of a more liquid nature in the doctrine of Christ and in the doctrine of the Trinity. The basis for these lies in an increasing understanding of more fluid notions of communion and relationship. Liquid church finds its resonance in these aspects of the faith and expresses them through the social organization of a network. The notion of a Church as network cannot be imposed by church organizations or created by mission agencies, or at least it cannot come about through the action of these groups on their own. A network-based liquid church must emerge from a connection to the spiritual desires and preferences of those who are so far outside of church life. In this sense it is related to sociological theory of consumption. How this link is made is set out in chapters 6 and 8.

A consumer culture, like any other culture, is a mixture of good and bad. This means that some aspects of it connect with the gospel and some do not. A fluid church could easily be a misguided, runaway church. There is therefore a need develop a theological framework within which a liquid church may have the freedom to flow. These limits are set out in chapter 7 and chapter 9. The first of these chapters deals with the doctrine of the Word of God and the second with the doctrine of the Holy Spirit. Finally, after this interconnected theological and sociological discussion, in chapter 10 I set out to describe what a liquid church might look like in practice.

WHAT IS CHURCH?

If the church may be described in theological and in sociological terms, then it is a challenge to know where to start in this discussion. It is hard to wear the two kinds of analytical hats at the same time, for in practice they exist together in a creative mix. On the page one generally has to switch from one to the other. This means it is tricky to know where to start. Chapter 1 is sociological, and this is a fair representation of the order of my thinking about the question of new forms of church. Given that fact, I want to conclude this introduction by discussing the nature of the church in theological terms. I will do this by reviewing Paul's use of the term *church* and the relationship between Jesus' preaching of the kingdom and the historical church. I have chosen to work with Paul's writings because they are some of the earliest in the New Testament, and their context is firmly located in the Christian communities that were emerging out of mission. The theology of the church has developed since Paul's time, and these other theological and cultural considerations will need to be taken into account as I argue for liquid church. The question of the kingdom of God and the church is important because it is the classic starting point for a revisionist discussion of the institution of the church, and liquid church is revisionist.

In the New Testament the Greek word *ekklesia* has generally been translated in two ways. The first is by the term *assembly*, and the second is by the word *church*. According to Kittel's *Theological Dictionary of the New Testament*, this latter definition has been variously interpreted, "depending upon denomination," as the whole church, the local congregation, or the house church.[4] J. D. G. Dunn treats the word in a similar way in his discussion of Paul's theology. For Paul the term church also refers to the "assembly of Yahweh." Dunn points out that this a remarkable move for the Jewish Paul, who connects the various Christian churches, which were made up primarily of non-Jewish believers, with the notion of Israel as the people of God.[5] Moreover, Paul identifies this wider assembly as characterizing the local community in a town or a city. "In short, there can be little doubt that Paul intended to depict the little assemblies of Christian believers as equally manifestations of and in direct continuity with 'the assembly of Yahweh,' 'the assembly of Israel.'"[6]

The notion of a universal church appears only in the later Pauline Epistles. In Col 1:18 Christ is the head of the wider body of the church. This does not necessarily mean that the local or the universal can be seen as opposing views within Pauline thought. Rather, the two exist together with a clear emphasis on the local community as the church of God.[7] At the same time the "church-ness" of the local community does not rely upon a link to a "universal church"; rather, this wider corporate reality—the people of God—depends upon a link to Christ and to the founding apostle.[8] The picture is complicated by Paul's evident willingness to regard the local community and much smaller house groups or house churches as also being the church of God. In 1 Cor 16:19 we see Paul sending greetings to "Aquila and Prisca, together with the church in their house." When 1 Cor 14:23 speaks of "the whole church" coming together, this indicates that regular gatherings may have consisted of a number of small groups meeting separately and that the wider congregational meeting would have been less frequent. He observes that these factors indicate the importance first of "assembly" as meeting together, but at the same time such meetings may have been quite small.

> Historically, it is a reminder of how dependent on quite tiny groups was the development of Christianity in the northeastern Mediterranean area. Theologically, the point is that the dynamic of being "the church of God" did not require large groups in any one place.[9]

The way that small groups and larger groups represent church in Paul's thought should lead us to be cautious about claiming too much for any present-day assertions about what

church should or should not be. The use of the word *church* in
Paul's writings does not indicate any one set pattern of community life that can guide us as we reimagine the church in our
context. Instead, when we examine the use of the word *ekklesia*
we are led to a web of interconnecting ideas related to the identity of the new, Gentile church. This identity is expressed at a
universal, a local, and a small-group level simultaneously. If,
however, we want the early church as our guide in developing a
liquid church, then it should lead us in one important direction. We see in Paul's writing that what it means to be church
cannot be contained in one clear social organization or institution. If we follow Paul, then we can regard a small group as
being just as much church as a townwide meeting. Linked to
this we can see that the church in a town like Corinth may have
been made up of a network of interconnecting and related
small groups. At the very least these insights should allow us to
critique some of our current approaches to church.

CHURCH AND KINGDOM

How we organize and think of church today is the result of
years of historical and social developments. The New Testament descriptions have been a theological starting point for
the church, but at various times the sociological pattern of
church life has had to be created and re-created. The historical
expression of what it means to be the assembly of God has
therefore gone through a series of changes and developments.
What this means is that the way we organize church may be in-
herited, but it is not preordained.

To suggest that we need a liquid church is not as radical as
it sounds; it is just another call for renewal and reformation.
One of the classic ways that this tension has been discussed
is to contrast the gospel of Jesus and the institution of the
church. As Alfred Loisy puts it, "Jesus proclaimed the kingdom of God, and what came was the Church."[10] This phrase
has been quoted so many times that it has perhaps lost some
of its power to shock. Yet it still contains a truth: the church, as
we experience it, often does not live up to the message of its
Lord. As individuals we fall short of the teaching of Jesus about
the kingdom of God. This is also the case with the church.
Loisy's observation implies that the kingdom offers an ideal of
the reign of God in the world, and we have put in its place an

institution. This basic insight causes us to take stock of what we are doing as God's people. It is an energy for reformation and renewal. At the same time the vision of the kingdom helps us to understand the church as part of God's ultimate plan for the world. The kingdom locates the church as part of what New Testament scholars call eschatology, or the study of the last things.

There has been considerable discussion among New Testament scholars concerning meaning of the kingdom of God in the teaching of Jesus.[11] A central question in this debate has been how much the kingdom of God is an event expected in the future and related to the end of the world (the *eschaton*) and how much it was instituted by the coming of Christ. Mark's Gospel opens with Jesus preaching that "the time is fulfilled, and the kingdom of God has come near; repent, and believe in the good news" (Mark 1:15). At the same time believers are encouraged to look forward and above all be prepared for the kingdom that will come in the future (Matt 8:11; 25:31–34). This means that the reign of God has commenced in Christ, but it is to be fulfilled at the end of time. Jesus leads us to the ultimate or last things, but now eschatology has to be stretched to a point where it has a beginning in Christ and an end in Christ.

The kingdom is the dynamic, kingly rule of God. It is also the arena within which this reign is experienced.[12] The kingdom is not identical with the church; rather, the kingdom creates the church. G. E. Ladd likens this to the parable in which the kingdom is described as being like a net that is dragged through the sea catching in its spread good and bad fish. The kingdom creates first the fellowship of Jesus' disciples and then the church, but neither is pure or perfect community.[13]

Individual Christians and the church exist in a tension between this "it is here now" and "it will soon be here" reality of life in the reign of God. The church is conditioned by the eschatological pattern of God's revealing of himself. Thus Hans Küng can say that: "Christian existence is lived between an indicative and an imperative, between present and future; the Christian community also lives in this tension, as the body of Christ and the people of God, as consecrated and yet sinful."[14] Küng points to how the sacraments of baptism and communion express this "inbetween-ness" of the church. They are simultaneously a remembrance of things that are past and an anticipation of what may come in the future. The church in the present expresses the life of God in the present, but this life is focused in Christ, who was and is and is to come. This eschatological, kingdom perspective serves to relativize our current expressions of church. The reign of God, says Küng, expresses the life-giving, healing, joyful glory of God. The problem is that because it is "in between" the church is also sinful and subject to mistakes and failures. The result is that most churches will fall short of the kingdom ideal.[15]

A LIQUID REFORMATION

The church must not stand still, because in every age it must seek to be a true expression of the kingdom. From time to time old patterns must be reviewed and renewed. I believe that we are in such a time.

Changes in contemporary culture have led many people to feel that church must again go through a period of innovation and change. In my view this is another kind of reformation. Far from resisting such change this brief excursion into the theology of the church appears to encourage a more open approach to the development of Christian communities. Paul's use of the word *ekklesia*, rather than exclusively supporting a solid congregational pattern of church life, might be seen as suggesting a more fluid or networked kind of community based on small groups. Alongside this the theology of the kingdom indicates that the organizational structures of the church should not be regarded as finalized or perfect. These insights allow us to approach the social structures of the church with a radical criticism, and that is just what we will do in the next two chapters.

Part One

SOLID CHURCH

Chapter 1

SOLID AND LIQUID MODERNITY
AND THE CHURCH

The question is whether our churches are part of the problem or part of the solution. When evangelism is discussed in books or at conferences there seems to be a growing appreciation that some version of church is vital for outreach in contemporary culture. Even if the ecclesiastical package offered comes in many forms—youth church, seeker church, church planting, emerging church, purpose-driven church, and so on—the common factor is the belief that church is the solution. The irony is that the search for the relevant church illustrates the extent to which church is still part of the problem. Why do we need to spend so much time and energy developing new forms of church if the ones we have are satisfactory? If church is part of the solution, then it is also part of the problem.

In many ways I share in the growing conviction that evangelism must pay more attention to the church. But it hasn't always been this way. For those engaged in evangelism and youth ministry forty or fifty years ago, the question of church was something of an irrelevance. Many parachurch agencies specifically set out to avoid the question of church. Organizations such as Young Life, Youth for Christ, or IVF (UCCF in the UK) have tended to see the question of church as a distraction from their primary mission of evangelism. Historically their aim has been to present a relevant gospel instead of a relevant church.[1] Communication of truth has been the priority. Today's evangelists and youth ministers share this interest, but they are starting to realize that a relevant gospel also requires a relevant church.

A simple reason exists for this change in priorities: we face a situation that didn't affect our forebears. We have an incredible opportunity, because we see that many people are searching for a spirituality; in the UK, young people may be more willing to become Christians than they have ever been. At the same time they appear to be increasingly reluctant to join our institutions.[2] They might have met Jesus, but they still don't want to meet the congregation! In parts of the US another phenomenon is at work. Young people are willing to attend youth fellowships, but when Sunday becomes Monday, they are all but indistinguishable in their behavior and in their beliefs, from their non-Christian peers at the high school. In these places youth ministry can look effective, but if we dig beneath the surface, problems emerge. In both of these cases a church that connects and makes a difference is needed. Yet to get the pattern of church life right, wherever we may be, we must understand why it does not work. It is hard to get the solution right if we have misunderstood the problem. To do this we need to examine development and changes in contemporary culture. This is where the term *liquid* becomes helpful.

LIQUID CULTURE

A number of thinkers have talked about contemporary culture in terms of a flexible or liquid modernity. David Lyon describes the impact of communication technologies and consumer culture as bringing about substantial changes in modernity. The new situation, he argues, is "mobile, mutable, fluid, flexible."[3] Ulrich Beck identifies what he calls "reflexive modernity,"[4] by which he means that modernity has turned its analytical skills in upon itself and has thereby created a less stable and more risk-filled environment. Discussing the change to an informational society, Manuel Castells focuses upon what he sees as a flexible and constantly changing environment. This flexibility shows itself in a variety of areas, including technological developments, organizational change, economics, and social structures.[5]

Constant technological change means that how we receive and process information is in a state of constant flux. The recent developments in how we can use mobile phones to do more than just talk to each other is good example. These technological changes produce an environment where we expect constantly to update or replace our communications equipment. The changes are so frequent that our relationship to technology has had to change to keep up. There's no point in

working our way through a manual that tells us how to operate
a technology. Instead we dive in and learn as we go. Nowadays
a computer program can do more than we need to do, so why
bother learning all about it? The situation is always changing,
and it isn't worth investing our time in comprehensive learning. A similar ambivalence operates in our relationship to
where we work. The new economy means that most of us
expect to change jobs on a regular basis. We will probably have
to retrain at least twice in our working lives. This fluid employment situation has led to people investing less in their identity
as employees of companies or even as a specific kind of skilled
worker.

In his discussion of cultural change Leonard Sweet also
uses the metaphor of liquid:

> If the Modern Era was a rage for order, regulation, stability,
> singularity, and fixity, the Postmodern Era is a rage for chaos,
> uncertainty, otherness, openness, multiplicity, and change. Post-
> modern surfaces are not landscapes but wavescapes, with the
> waters always changing and the surfaces never the same. The sea
> knows no boundaries.[6]

Sweet believes that we need to develop a church that can
negotiate what he describes as an "aquaculture" of postmodernity.[7] The prevailing ecclesial image in Sweet's work is
that of the boat. The Bible becomes a kind of maritime chart,
and the minister is the ship's captain or pilot. Sweet's imagery
is similar to mine, in that he uses a liquid metaphor to describe the contemporary cultural situation. He is right to pick
up on sociological thinking that speaks of contemporary culture as fluid or flexible, but we part company in the metaphor
of the boat. This image seems to imply that we can create a
church that can float upon the waves and ultimately keep its
passengers dry. Moreover, saying that we are in new and un-
charted waters might lead the church to treat culture as an
obstacle to be overcome or a problem to be solved.

Liquid church, in contrast, starts from the positive ele-
ments in the new, fluid environment and tries to work with
these and make them part of the way forward for the church.
We need to develop ways of being a church that doesn't float
on water like a boat. To be a liquid church means that we
are able to combine with water to become fluid, changeable,
flexible, and so on. We need to embrace and internalize the

liquid nature of culture rather than to learn to sail through it. Only by locating church within culture can we find ways to develop a distinctive Christian expression within that culture.

SOLID AND LIQUID

In *Liquid Modernity*[8] Zygmunt Bauman explores the changes in contemporary culture. He distinguishes between what he calls solid or "heavy" modernity and liquid modernity. He suggests that the modern world came out of the medieval feudal society through a process of questioning and replacing previous certainties. This process was originally seen as a kind of melting of the solids. So, he says, modernity emerges from the untying of the economy from traditional and religious linkages. Production is disconnected from a sense of obligation to the institutions of the family and the church. Thus ties of commitment to the home and to the sacred are replaced by a more rational system of organization and order.[9] The factory, the office, modern government, and institutional bureaucracy all exhibit signs of this shift from traditional to a "modern" and a more rational order. In time, however, these systems are themselves regarded as restrictive. Modernity substitutes one solid for another, this being a solid built from the sum of individual choosing. Solid modernity is based on the victory of the settled over the nomad; it is a culture of production rather than consumption and above all is linked to ways of organizing production that were first developed by the car maker Henry Ford. Modernity was shaped by the Fordist principles of expansion, size, plant, boundaries, norms, rules, and class-orientated affinities and identities.[10]

Now, says Bauman, modernity is undergoing a liquifying process. Central to this change is the way that capital has been released from location. "In its heavy stage, capital was as much fixed to the ground as were the laborers it engaged. Nowadays capital travels light—with cabin baggage only, which includes no more than a briefcase, a cellular phone and a portable computer."[11] Changes in productive processes mean that individuals can no longer expect to follow a safe career within one organization. Changes in technology and working arrangements have meant that an identity located in being a company employee or in a particular skill or trade becomes less feasible. At the same time large social collectives based on class and identity have been eroded. A flexible workforce is made up of individual consumers who find their identity in how they live rather than social class. Who we are is something to be achieved rather than to be learned. The individual has to shape identity apart from community. In all of this, consumption is privileged over production: I am what I buy rather than what I do.[12] For individuals and for the wider processes of production the solidity of modernity has given way to a new arena that is characterized by increased flexibility and constant change. To describe this as a liquid modernity seems appropriate.

Solid Church

Solid modernity has spawned a solid form of church that has internalized some of the core values of modernity in its early phase. So, just as we can talk of solid modernity, it is equally possible to discuss solid church. Solid church does not refer to one distinct way of being a Christian community. It is not possible to point to one denomination or theology and say it originated solid church. Rather, across the denominations and in many nondenominational groups it is possible to identify a pattern of tendencies. These tendencies together illustrate aspects of what it is to be solid church.

Attendance at Church Services Equals Faithfulness

In the game show *The Weakest Link* contestants are asked questions in turn. A correct answer gives a certain amount of money to the individual, but this money must be banked if it is to form part of the eventual prize. Solid church has its eyes firmly on the bank. The local church may support many good and important activities, including mission trips, evangelism, youth ministry, social projects, and so on, but they are all assessed in terms of their effect or otherwise on regular Sunday attendance. People may have turned to Christ through the youth mission or Alpha course, and this is good, but they are not banked, they don't really count, until they start to attend Sunday services.

Congregation characterizes solid church. By congregation I mean the tendency to emphasize one central meeting. Usually this meeting is a worship service held weekly on a Sunday morning. Gathering in one place to do the same thing together

is one of the core values of solid church. Despite the evident
interest in developing new ways of church, the basic assumption that we must form congregations has not been challenged. Even where we run separate youth churches or youth
worship services,[13] in effect we develop the same kind of congregational entity for one segment of the church. The congregation is king in solid church.

I have sometimes felt that the real purpose of church services is to enable clergy to count the congregation. This is
probably a little cynical, but solid church finds its main sense
of success in the number of people who attend on a Sunday.
Regular church attendance is seen as being a significant test of
spiritual health, and church growth is measured in terms of
the size of congregations. The importance of Sunday attendance and congregational size can never be underestimated
for solid church.

Bauman describes the factory system of solid modernity
as being like a panopticon. The panopticon, invented by Jeremy
Bentham, is a circular prison with layer upon layer of cells fac-
ing in toward the center of the circle. From one side of this
prison the guards can observe the every movement of the pris-
oners and check to see if they follow the prescribed routine.
Bauman observes that the panopticon does not just restrict
the prisoner; it also imprisons the guards.[14] The same is true
for the relationship between managers and workers in the factory system. Both are locked into a relationship of checking
and being checked.

Solid church represents similar restriction of those in the
congregation and of those running the services. The emphasis
upon attendance at one central service enables ministers to
see easily if people are starting to flag in their spiritual lives.
We might attend to hear the preacher, but clergy often attend
because they want to see us there. The system of counting the
sheep and making sure they attend can lead us into unhealthy
relationships of surveillance and control. Ministers sometimes
express frustration with the way that a central service restricts
their ability to experiment and be creative, and the weight of
being responsible for the regular attendance of members can
be intolerable. As a youth minister in a church I felt something
of this pressure. When the numbers of young people sitting
in back pew increased I was doing well, but if they started
to decrease, questions were asked. The implication was that

it was my job to look after their spiritual health, and this was assessed in terms of their regular attendance on Sunday mornings.

Size Counts

In solid modernity the size of the factory building was a major sign of success. Extending the production facility was the aim of business. Similarly solid church focuses on building bigger buildings to hold more people and process more activities. Megachurches are springing up around the fringes of American suburbs, each a witness to the success of that particular congregation and senior pastor. Churches such as Willow Creek have developed a line of activity based on people who want to learn the secret of growing one of these huge churches. In the UK, with its historic buildings, such megacongregations are almost nonexistent. Instead, the successful church extends its influence by developing a new outlet in a nearby location: a church plant.

Church planting has become a way of growing the influence and market share of the congregation. Church plants may be distinctive from the mother church, or they may be identical in many ways. Still the DNA will contain congregation as its basic ingredient. For church plant we could read congregation plant, because most have a central meeting for worship at the core.

One Size Fits All

The logic of mass production is standardization of product and services. It's Henry Ford's maxim, "You can have any color car as long as it's black." Solid church is based on the assumption that it is good for large numbers of very different people to meet in the same room and do the same sort of thing together. Worship therefore becomes a one-size-fits-all environment. The result is that we provide a rather bland and inoffensive diet of middle-of-the-road music and safe spirituality. Variety in what we have to offer is severely limited by the tastes and prejudices of those who attend. Extremes are tempered because one of the key values is that we do not offend anyone who comes to church regularly. One or two critical comments will prompt the leaders of the church to tell the youth group to turn the instruments down!

One size fits all is made into a virtue by those who run
solid church. Everything about regular Sunday worship is designed to make us feel that even if we don't like it, we should
still attend because it is good for us. As with cough medicine,
we endure the bad taste because we are told that it is doing
us good.

Join the Club

Like a local golf or tennis club, where active members keep
the club going through a series of time-consuming commit-
tees, the church has become an exclusive club run for its
members and organized by a team of voluntary helpers. Long-
term service gives a degree of authority and deference on the
part of others. For many key club members, organizing the
club becomes an end in itself.

In our towns and cities, innumerable groups and associations function in similar ways. Such clubs offer individuals a
place where they can find a sense of purpose and identity.
They represent a social world that is like a small pond where
one or two people can be big fish and a few others can find
safety and security in the sunny waters.

Solid church, like these clubs, has become a place where
some people find a sense of self and significance by giving
themselves in voluntary activity. The congregation is also
very like a pond, a self-contained world where people can
feel secure and that they belong. It is worth thinking for
a while of all the various roles and activities associated
with the average church. Keeping the solid church running
is a major activity demanding continual effort and activity
not just from the paid staff but more importantly from the
volunteers. This activity is made into a virtue, and it is part
of what it means to be a faithful member. With people safely
assigned to a particular role, leaders can feel that they are fulfilling themselves and that they have a sense of loyalty and
commitment from the congregation. Clergy therefore make
it their task to try to get people "more involved" in helping
out in one way or another. Solid church makes voluntary activity in the organization part of the package of Christian discipleship. If you want spiritual experience or intimacy with
fellow believers, then this comes only as part of a lifetime
of service.

MODERNITY AND THE CHURCH

Our churches are not immune from the influence of contemporary culture. The importance of attendance at church services, the emphasis on planting more churches, the one-size-fits-all worship, and the development of church life as a kind of club all indicate the extent to which church has internalized solid modernity. These tendencies I have labeled solid church.

The ability to connect with modernity in the various ways has been a significant factor in the life and energy of today's church. The challenge for solid church is that culture has started to change toward a much more fluid form of modernity. When the waters are moving all around it, solid church finds itself in a very different place. We might think that we are doing the same kind of things that we have always done, but cultural change affects us whether we like it or not. Few if any of us are immune from cultural change. We share a common liquid culture. This means that we not only see the church differently; we also relate to it differently. So while solid church looks roughly the same as it always has, under the surface it too has started to change and mutate. In the next chapter we'll observe the mutations of solid church.

Chapter 2

THE MUTATIONS OF SOLID CHURCH: HERITAGE, REFUGE, AND NOSTALGIA

Solid church has emerged from solid modernity as a successful way of being church. The one-size-fits-all congregation-based institution of the local church represents a realistic attempt to create a viable Christian community in the first phase of modernity. The problem is that this predictable phase has started to change all around us. Certainties become more fuzzy as modernity becomes more liquid. Personal identity has become a more disputed territory than was previously the case, moral certainties have been shown to be a matter of debate, pervious ideas about what it means to be American or British have to be readjusted in the light of our increasingly multicultural and multiethnic populations. All of these are examples of the way that the contemporary experience of life is less fixed or certain—in other words, liquid. This has created a new context for the church. The challenge of the liquid environment is not simply that people experience life in new ways and so we have to find new ways to reach them. The real challenge of liquid modernity is that it has affected the church. This chapter examines the way that changes in modernity have affected solid church. These changes or mutations are positive in that they explain why some churches succeed in the current climate but negative in that while these churches are meaningful and positive places for some people, they are at the same time an obstacle to others finding faith. The irony is that both these positive and negative effects result from the mutations I describe.

COMMUNITY IDENTITY AND BELONGING

Social, economic, and cultural change has affected the nature of the church. If we examine three patterns of society—

premodern (thirteenth to sixteenth centuries), modern (seventeenth to the mid-twentieth centuries), and postmodern or liquid (mid-twentieth century to the present)—it is possible to describe some basic changes in the way that the church's community life was structured.[1] In premodern societies, with economies located mainly on the land, communal life was based around a sense of place. So the idea of a parish expresses the way that the church served all of those, rich and poor, those who worked on the land and those who owned the land. Community, organized around the village or the small town, was inclusive, even if it was not always equitable.

The modern era was characterized by a significant change in the way that community and identity were experienced. With emigration, urbanization, and industrialization the parish became less significant. Community became relocated in various gathered groupings based on culture and shared experience. In this context solid church emerged with its emphasis on congregation and club as place of identity and significance for Christians. The church incorporated certain values from the surrounding culture, and so we eventually see the development of church as a plant where size and numbers are determining factors.

The liquid or postmodern era reshapes the notion of identity and therefore of community in significant ways. Anthony Giddens suggests that in the current phase of what he terms "high modernity," identity construction becomes more complex and less certain. The world in which we live "creates new forms of fragmentation and dispersal."[2] Thus he describes what he calls "the reflexive project of the self."[3]

> . . . because of the "openness" of social life today, the pluralization of contexts of action and the diversity of "authorities," lifestyle choice is increasingly important in the constitution of self-identity and daily activity. Reflexively organized life planning, which normally presumes consideration of risks as filtered through contact with expert knowledge, becomes a central feature of the structuring of self-identity.[4]

People are reflexive because they continually review their sense of self in relation to the increasing number of choices available in society. The fact that there are many choices leads to a certain amount of insecurity. In solid modernity, individual identity was securely located in class and gender norms. So tightly prescribed were these roles that escape was not much easier than it had been in the premodern world of social class structures and the notion of divine order. In the rapidly changing, fluid environment of the present, however, these identity options are no longer in play. This means that individuals do not feel constrained by them, but neither are they there as a possible source of retreat and security.[5] People face life's challenges and problems on their own. In the past it was possible to translate social contradictions into collective struggles, but this is no longer a viable option.[6] The consequent individualization of risk and identity formation means that we are responsible for our own success or failure. The result, says Zygmunt Bauman, is that we are now individuals seeking a precarious way forward in an environment of increasing choice with little guidance or direction.

> What emerges from the fading social norms is naked, frightened aggressive ego in search of love and help. In the search for itself and an affectionate sociality, it easily gets lost in the jungle of the self. . . . Someone who is poking around in the fog of his or her own self is no longer capable of noticing that this isolation, this solitary confinement of the ego is a "mass sentence."[7]

The plight of the individual seeking to establish an enduring sense of self in the shifting waters of liquid modernity leads to significant changes in the way that community operates. Previous possibilities from the modern or premodern era are no longer viable, says Bauman. Instead, respite is sought in what he variously calls "peg," "cloakroom," or "carnival" communities. Peg communities offer the chance for individuals to gather for a moment around a "nail" on which they can peg their individual fears.[8] Cloakroom communities allow individuals to dress for an event, leave their coats at the door, and enjoy a temporary spectacle. A carnival is similarly a gathering of individuals around an event that offers a brief distraction from the demands and fears of a fluid, unsettled search for identity and meaning.[9]

Bauman sees the attempt to develop community in liquid modernity as something of an illusion. At best it is some kind of shelter, an "island of homely and cozy tranquility in a sea of turbulence and inhospitality."[10] Those seeking such shelter do so "in spite" of what is happening around them.

In the more fluid context of liquid modernity, how individuals gain a sense of self in relation to others is in a constant state of change. This means that the possibility of community becomes much more problematic. For solid church this new environment is particularly problematic.

THE MUTATING CHURCH

Solid church does not disappear in liquid modernity; rather, it experiences a subtle mutation. Just as in modernity the premodern aspects of the church continued, so in liquid modernity the premodern, parish-based church and the modern congregation or gathered church also continue. But while they may still exist, they do not remain unchanged by the fluidity of people's lives and the surrounding culture. Liquid modernity brings about mutation in the parish and in the congregation. These changes have emerged almost imperceptibly, so much so that many church leaders may not have noticed what has happened. Those running parishes and congregations think that they are doing what the church has always done. Unfortunately neither the congregation nor the people in the wider parish have stood still. Liquid modernity has seeped under the church door and into the sanctuary.

The fluid nature of contemporary culture means that the local parish no longer exists. Of course the geographical area still exists, but the relationships between individuals and groups that made up what it means to be a local community have substantially altered. The links between landowners, laborers, and clergy that marked the premodern parish have disappeared. A similar observation can be made of the social collectives of working-class urban workers or European immigrants to the US that gave birth to the congregational model of church life. For writers such as Bauman these changes mean that community as it was once experienced no longer exists.

This change in community at a local and a collective level has made churches mutate. Whereas once they reflected a social reality beyond themselves, now this is less likely to be the case. This means that since church does not reflect a wider community it must in some way compensate for this lack. At the same time those who attend church do so with a different set of social needs. Now church is seen as a personal lifestyle choice alongside many others. Moreover, which church we go to in a particular town is also seen as a matter of choice. In a culture dominated by ways of consuming, solid church finds that in order to be successful it must adjust. As a result churches have gradually adapted to a new, more fluid market environment while generally denying that such changes have taken place. The result of this is that mutation has adapted the church to relate to some to the needs of those who are willing or able to fit their basic pattern, but they are unable or unwilling to change this solid way of being church to connect with those who find it unacceptable or unattractive.

Solid church generally mutates in three ways: as heritage site, as refuge, and as nostalgic community. These are ways of describing a complex and organic process that can be observed happening in churches in the UK and the US. No one church mutates in exactly the same way, and many times these individual mutations combine into a cocktail of adaptations to contemporary, fluid culture. The adaptations are driven by the need of church leaders to attract numbers and the desire of those who already belong to church to find a place of significance and meaning in an uncertain cultural environment.

Church as Heritage Site

In the premodern era the worship of the church was part of a common culture. In sixteenth-century England, when Archbishop Thomas Cranmer wrote the Anglican prayer book, it was called *The Book of Common Prayer.* The language of the prayer book and of the King James Bible helped to shape what it meant to be English. The worship in the local church was a communal worship for all of the people who lived within the boundaries of the parish. In the modern era the worship of the church was much more closely related to people groups. So we see the importance of *The Methodist Hymn Book* for communities in Wales or the significance of the preaching of Puritans for the early settlers in New England. In the premodern and modern eras, church tradition was decisively shaped by the effect of economic and social forces on the formation of communities.

In liquid modernity, church tradition of all kinds has been dislocated from its former communal roots. The parish no longer functions as an expression of community. People's lives are now so mobile that their connection to place has been significantly altered. Similarly with the links between particular groups and styles of worship; the range of lifestyle choices has eroded the connection between particular groups and Christian worship. Social change has left many churches locked in a cultural time warp.

As living expressions of worship from another era, church has taken on a historical character. Far from being a turn-off, for some people the weekly visit to church is attractive precisely because it offers a slice of living history. Worship has become part of the culture industry. The value of church is that it preserves the traditions of the past and makes them accessible to new generations. Many of these traditions are seen as being culturally worthy. The music of the church choir and the organ has an aesthetic of high art. The architecture and literature of the church are prized as being artistically significant. For those attending worship, keeping the heritage site going is much like any other historical preservation society. It becomes a passion and a place of investment financially and in terms of identity.

As the tradition of the church is mutated by liquid modernity, the minister slowly turns into curator. Historical conservation is moderated by the need to accommodate the present congregation. Ministers and people are willing to see gradual change, but every effort is made to respect the weight of tradition. In all of this the church is very like any other conservation trust dealing with historic monument or stately home. The emphasis lies upon preserving for future generations that with which we have been entrusted.

Church as Refuge

The new, fluid modernity offers little support or shelter in the face of overwhelming change and almost unlimited choice. In these circumstances individuals look for welcoming places where they can find a sense of togetherness and safety. When the sense of a wider community has all but eroded, solid church develops into a place of refuge where we retreat for a while. In home groups, Sunday school classes, social activities, youth ministries, and social programs we meet people who share our values. In refuge church we are encouraged to feel that to be a Christian is to be part of wider family group. To feed belonging, the church has increasingly diversified into christianized versions of the wider culture, so church has a basketball team, a golf fellowship, a youth ministry with its own band. Christian parents encourage their children to watch Christian movies and send their children to private Christian schools or homeschool them. Through the church we might have access to a born-again economy of Christian stores, plumbers, lawyers, gardeners, and web designers. In the refuge church we feel that if we do business with a committed Christian we may be safer.

The bigger the shelter, the more comfortable it becomes, and the more people it can accommodate. So we see churches working in every way possible to develop different ways of attracting people into their community. As some churches have become more and more attractive to people they transform from refuge and become a resort. No longer does the church give emergency cover in a time of trouble; now it is able to present itself as an attractive place for a vacation. And as is the case in every holiday resort, some people find a way to live there year round.

Church as Nostalgic Community

Although it is closely related to refuge and heritage, this mutation of the church relates to its conception of itself rather than its reality. The church as nostalgic community appeals to an imagined past. There is a kind of lament for what existed in the connection between congregation and social groups in the modern congregation or for the close relationship between the experience of worshipers in the church and the social geography of the church community. With liquid modernity loosening both of these kinds of communal ties, a yearning for a previous age develops. This yearning is essentially nostalgic, because it does not account for either the economic or the social factors that produced the churches of modernity and premodernity. The nostalgic community sells itself as the one place where communal meetings remain possible in society. We tell ourselves that in church young and old gather together in ways they never do outside of church. This kind of myth makes us feel good about our congregation.

The nostalgic community of the church is more wish fulfillment than reality. Congregations are generally monocultures reflecting the tastes of one or perhaps two different types of people. Black and white most often worship separately, as do

the working class and the middle class. Yet the nostalgic community is extremely powerful because it is one of the myths
the church believes about itself.

WHY WE NEED A LIQUID CHURCH

The mutations of parish- and congregation-based church
indicate that liquid modernity will not sweep away the existing church. When ice turns to water, for a substantial period
it exists as solid and liquid. We should expect to see solid
and liquid types of church develop in response to cultural
change.[11]

This is similarly the case with solid and liquid modernity.
What we describe is not a postmodernity, that is, a time when
modernity has come to an end. Liquid modernity melts parts
of solid modernity and leaves other parts still fairly solid.
These too are the mutations of solid church. They look sort of
the same, but they too have been affected by the changes in
contemporary culture. One reason for this is that some characteristics of modernity remain helpful and useful. Paddy
Scannell points out that in the average store the range of toast-
ers is limited to a few basic colors and functions. We don't
require significant individual design in such a kitchen gadget.
He calls this the "for anyone" structure of modernity, and typi-
cally mass-produced goods exhibit these standardizing characteristics.[12] When we travel by train or when we visit the
dentist we expect a reliable, regular, and safe service, deliv-
ered by professionals for the right price. We want solid, rational modernity when it comes to travel and health care.

Solid modernity is still with us and has its place even if it is
surrounded by its own melted contents. The same should be
the case with solid church. I do not argue that we should abandon all existing patterns of church in favor of this new idea or
proclaim that all is "post" and that this heralds an impending
apocalypse that will sweep solid church before it. I do suggest
two things.

First, the mutation of solid church into heritage, refuge,
and nostalgic communities has seriously decreased its ability
to engage in genuine mission in liquid modernity. These mutations degrade the gospel genetic code of the church. This
means that what is offered in our churches and more importantly what many people seek has been devalued to a greater

or lesser extent. Solid church has found ways to adapt to the new environment, but these adaptations have left it with a limited repertoire of communal reflexes. By offering refuge to some, solid church fails to find ways to connect to the liquid search of others. By claiming to be community, it often struggles to find ways to be the kingdom of God in the wider society. Solid church, by ignoring the fluid nature of culture, has found itself stranded on a desert island. This island is pleasant; it has a rich supply of fruit and hospitable inhabitants. Yet, this haven is built on shaky foundations, for behind some people's refuge and retreat lies a much more shady reality. As long as the solid church responds to contemporary culture by presenting itself as one of these mutations, it will sell itself short. Isolated on its beach, all it can do is try to entice others to join it. The possibility of engaging in mission within the surrounding culture becomes increasingly problematic because in seeking refuge it has been forced to present itself as in some way separated from ordinary life.

Second, liquid church is essential because it takes the present culture seriously and seeks to express the fullness of the Christian gospel within that culture. Solid church has mutated because it has ignored cultural change, and as a result it has found itself to be changed in ways that are less than planned or perfect. In catering to the religious needs of some, it has as a consequence failed to respond to the wider spiritual hunger. Solid church will continue to change and adapt to contemporary culture, and in many places people will find ways to develop distinctive styles of mission and evangelism. At the same time the mutant genetic code within these kinds of churches means that they are a poor starting point for a new kind of church that connects with the liquid flow of spiritual hunger evident in our societies. To do this we need to start afresh with a liquid church Reformation.

Part Two

LIQUID CHURCH

Chapter 3

LIQUID IN CHRIST

What does it mean to be a liquid church? Is it possible to conceive of a Christian community that is not structured around congregation and a central meeting? A congregationless church seems unthinkable. Is it possible to be a flexible and fluid church that also remains faithful to the gospel and to the traditions of the faith? The following chapters will examine how a liquid church can respond to changes in contemporary culture. The sociological argument will be discussed in chapters 4, 6 and 8. The theological basis for liquid church will be set out in the chapters that fall between these (chs. 3, 5, and 7). Our starting point will be once again theological, with a discussion of the doctrine of Christ.

CHRIST AND THE CHURCH

The reality of the church is to be found only in Christ. Christ is our origin and our truth.[1] To be a Christian is to be joined to Christ, and to be joined to Christ is to be joined to his church. As Timothy Bradshaw puts it, "The church is the church of Jesus Christ and all individual Christians are united in him."[2]

A couple of conclusions follow from this basic theological principle. First, any kind of church, liquid or otherwise, must find its origin in a union with Christ. Christians are first joined to Christ, and this connection makes them one with each other. Second, while acknowledging the effects of a consumer culture and embracing some of its aspects, liquid church must give shape to the corporate nature of what it means to be "in Christ." This chapter will lay the theological foundations for liquid church by looking at Paul's theology of participation in Christ.

IN CHRIST

The phrase "in Christ" and its various related formulations are a characteristic of Paul's presentation of the Christian

gospel. This expression is so pervasive that alongside "justifi-
cation by faith" the notion of participation in Christ represents an organizing metaphor in Paul's theology.[3] At its most
basic the phrase "in Christ" is used in relation to the events of
salvation:

> So if anyone is in Christ, there is a new creation: everything old
> has passed away; see, everything has become new! (2 Cor 5:17)

To be "in Christ" is to be made anew, to be re-created. But
this subjective experience of salvation, says G. E. Ladd, should
be understood in relation to the wider eschatological framework of Paul's thinking. To be "in Christ" is related to Paul's
notion of all people being "in Adam."[4] Thus Paul can say, "As
all die in Adam, so all will be made alive in Christ" (1 Cor
15:22). Those who are "in Adam" belong to the old era of sin
and death. Those who are in Christ are united to him in his
death and resurrection and so are made alive.[5] The new life
in Christ has come and also is yet to come. Thus Paul can say
that "in Christ God was reconciling the world to himself"
(2 Cor 5:19) and that believers "will be made alive in Christ"
(1 Cor 15:22).[6]

J. D. G. Dunn divides the users of the phrase "in Christ"
into three groups. The first, which he calls the "objective
usage," echoes Ladd's account of the eschatological work of
Christ.[7] The second use of "in Christ" is more subjective in
character; in such passages Paul speaks of believers "being" in
Christ. This is the personal effect of the work of Christ in the
individual believer. Believers are those "sanctified in Christ"
(1 Cor 1:2), are "all one in Christ" (Gal 3:28), and are encouraged to reckon themselves as being dead to sin and made alive
in Christ (Rom 6:11).[8] The third group of phrases refers to
Paul's ministry as being "in Christ." So Paul writes to the
Corinthians that he speaks "in Christ" (2 Cor 2:17). Paul's various uses of "in Christ" indicate that alongside belief about
Christ there is also an experience "of the risen and living
Christ." Both of these are important aspects of Paul's thinking.[9] Paul felt that he had been taken up in the life of Christ
and from now on his life was linked to that of Christ.

Closely related to being "in Christ" is Paul's idea that
Christ also indwells the believer. For example, in Galatians
Paul says, "I have been crucified with Christ; and it is no longer

I who live, but it is Christ who lives in me" (Gal 2:19–20). In the later Pauline Epistles we read that Christ in us is the "hope of glory" (Col 1:27), and in Eph 3:17 the prayer is that Christ may "dwell in your hearts through faith." All of this indicates that Paul sees our union with Christ as his presence surrounding and indwelling the believer. This relationship sustains and establishes the believer in relationship with God, but also it forges a wider community base to faith. The shared experience of the Lord unites into one body all of those who are in Christ.[10]

IN THE BODY OF CHRIST

The body is the dominant image in Paul's theology of the church.[11] This metaphor is used in 1 Cor 10 and 12 and in Colossians and in Ephesians. Paul's use of the body as a metaphor for the church draws upon the widespread first-century use of this image for the city or the state.[12] The metaphor of the body would have been more familiar to his readers.[13] Dunn argues that in the imagery of the body, Paul progresses from a picture of the Christian community that is based upon the nation-state (of Israel) to one that connects with the local community or body politic. Thus in his letter to the Romans Paul moves swiftly from the idea of Israel as the people of God, by way of the notion of sacrifice, to speaking of the body in Rom 12:5. In Paul's vision of the body of Christ, unity does not arise from living in the same place; rather, it comes from a common allegiance or connection to Christ. As Dunn says:

> The identity of the Christian assembly as "body," however, is given not by geographical location or political allegiance but by their common allegiance to Christ (visibly expressed not least in baptism and the sacramental sharing in his body).[14]

The body of Christ is seen as a charismatic community. In Romans and in 1 Corinthians this is expressed in terms of charisms. The charism is a result of the gracious gift of God. According to Dunn it is closely related to *charis* and is a "concrete materialization of God's grace."[15] The gifts of God are related in 1 Cor 12 to a parallel range of diverse acts of service. As such individuals are expected to be active, their activity is to be for the common good.[16] The basic imagery of the body of Christ connects diversity with unity. Difference is expressed in

terms of the activity of the various members and the gifts of
service and ministry that they contribute to the Christian
church. Each member is not just an individual; members are
to be joined to the body and expected to contribute in a particular way depending upon their gifts.[17]

The body of Christ is constituted by the gift of the Spirit.
Through baptism and the working of the Spirit individual
believers are made as one "in Christ." Startlingly, we are told
that unity in Christ transcends racial and social barriers; to
have drunk of the Spirit is to be made one. So Paul can say,
"For in the one Spirit we were all baptized into one body—
Jews or Greeks, slaves or free—and we were all made to drink
of the one Spirit" (1 Cor 12:12). Reflecting on this verse, C. K.
Barrett observes that baptism in this sense should be seen a
process of joining to Christ and thus to all the other believers
who are also joined to him.[18] As such the unity of the Spirit was
something given to believers. The fellowship of believers has
not been created by human action; it has come through a
mutual sharing in the life of the Spirit.

In Christ or in Church

Believers are one with each other because they are joined
to Christ. The temptation is to reverse these priorities, so that
by being joined to the church one is joined to Christ. But connection to Christ through baptism and the drinking of the
Spirit should take precedence over any ecclesiastical pattern.
This does not mean that the social or liturgical life of the
church may not be a means to conversion. However, the reason for prioritizing union with Christ is that it makes room for
new ways of being church.

Paul's use of the phrase "in Christ" shifts us beyond an
institutionally bound church life. We are "in Christ" when
what we do and say accord with his character and his life. We
are in Christ when we experience the directing and guiding of
the Holy Spirit. We are "in Christ" when we worship and celebrate together. The Christ in whom we dwell and who dwells
in us pervades all of life and surrounds the world with his
energy and presence. As the writer to the Colossians says, this
Christ was the "firstborn of all creation." Through him all
things were made, and through him all things were reconciled
to God (Col 1:15). If we say that we are joined to Christ, then

this must mean that we too are linked to the dynamic, flowing energy of God in the world.

It is worth reflecting for a moment on the difference between these ideas of what it means to be "in Christ" and what immediately comes to mind when we use the phrase "in church." When we say "in church," it is hard to get some kind of building out of our minds. This imagery is the heart of the debate about liquid church. We need to find some way of imagining church that reflects the fullness of Christ in whom all things join together. Paul was able to combine a dynamic lifestyle of being in Christ with the idea of being one with other Christians in the body of Christ. For us these two ideas often seem to be miles away from each other, and yet if we were able to make this shift, then a whole new way of being "in Christ" and in the body of Christ will be opened to us. This is what I mean when I speak of the church as liquid. It is an attempt to reach out beyond what it means to be "in church" and toward what it means to be caught up in the liquid life of Christ.

THE BODY OF CHRIST

To be joined to Christ is to be joined to the body of Christ. This corporate and corporeal expression of Christ is fundamental to any theology of the church. The idea of the body of Christ goes very deep in people's minds. Yet it is worth reflecting on how we express this truth, for to say that the body of Christ is the church is not the same as saying that the church is the body of Christ. The implication of my reading of Paul's theology is that we should place significantly more emphasis upon the way that our connection to Christ makes us part of the body, rather than the other way around. When I have given lectures on liquid church this distinction has been one of the key points in dispute. Most people are concerned to oppose what they see as the individualism of contemporary society. One clergyman expressed this to me by talking about postmodern culture as consumer-based and fragmented. In contrast he saw the church as being a community in opposition to what he said were "destructive forces." He was very disturbed that I appeared to challenge his idea of the existing church as corporate and community, and he couldn't see how a liquid network of communication could fulfill his vision of what it means to be the body of Christ. His objection to liquid church, I wanted to explain, was based on a misunderstanding. I am not abandoning the church as a community in favor of fragmented individualism. What I do suggest is that there are different and more cultural expressions of what this corporate body of Christ might look like.

The problem is that most Christians see an inevitable link between the church as local and national institution and the theological designation "the body of Christ." There is a vital truth to this; the church is the body of Christ. At the same time, however, the failure to reverse the order and say that the body of Christ is the church means that we are often unable to imagine ourselves outside of the institutional box. This imagining, however, is fundamental to liquid church. Here we reverse the order and say that we are joined to Christ and therefore joined to each other, and as we express this corporate life of Christ we are church. This idea of church is being constantly reformed, transformed, shaped, and reshaped. Relationships, groups, and communication are fundamental, for through the connections made between people the church is formed. As individuals find their unity with each other in Christ, the networks develop. Worship, prayer, and mission flow from these dynamic connections. This is far from embracing fragmentation and individualism. We are not, however, accepting that church, as it is at the moment, is the only way to express the corporate Christ.

PARTICIPATION AND DIFFERENCE

Paul's vision of those joined to Christ as one body carries within it a significant emphasis upon difference as well as unity. As eyes, ears, feet, and so on, each member within the body plays a distinctive and yet important role. These differences are presented as fundamental and nonnegotiable, but together they are used to generate the life of the body as a whole. Basic to this argument is the way that each part of the body plays a part for the greater good. We all need each other, but more importantly we must all fulfill our function. From this analogy it seems clear that those joined to Christ are expected to be different. In fact Paul encourages them to express their differences for the mutual benefit of one another.

Within many churches this aspect of the body of Christ has been expressed through the idea of every-member ministry. Liquid church extends this idea and again reverses its sequence. Instead of church being a place where everyone can have a ministry, liquid church emerges out of the active ministry of everyone who is joined to Christ. As people join to Christ and communicate Christ with one another, the networked pattern that grows from this faithful communication of believers is then identified as church.

JOINED TO THE LIQUID CHRIST

Paul's habitual reference to the Christian life as being in Christ takes us deep into his theological imagination. He sees life as being lived in communion with Christ. This is not simply individualized spiritual experience, because the connection to Christ initiates a connection with one another. This is a theological argument about the priority of ideas. Liquid church takes this theoretical framework and uses it to allow new forms of church to emerge. Along the way it takes the core values of participation in the body, the value of difference, the inevitability of community, and the way that these are rooted in the experience of Christ and the work of the Holy Spirit.

Chapter 4

NETWORK AND FLOW IN THE LIQUID CHURCH

A liquid is characterized by flow. Flow means that the particles in a liquid move over each other freely so that the liquid can appear to be continually on the move. This flow means that a quantity of liquid has no shape of its own (see "liquid" in the *Shorter Oxford English Dictionary*). In contrast, a solid does not move in the same way; its shape is located and firm. Shape or solidity, says Zygmunt Bauman, can be seen as the equivalent of "fixing space" and "binding time."[1] Solids are able to "neutralize the effects of time." This means that in describing a solid shape we do not need to discuss the way that it changes shape or moves. Change and movement make sense only when we introduce time as a factor. An example of this would be if I tried to describe the way that the strange glutinouslike substance starts to move when my daughter turns on the lava lamp in her bedroom. My description would have to be something like this: "First it was a round, egglike shape, and then a large piece broke off and began to float up toward the top of the lamp. And then that piece formed a heart shape, and so on." The repeated use of "and then" is essential because, like all fluids, the lava in the lamp constantly changes. This can be expressed only by the use of some notion of time. When we discuss a solid, time is of little importance, says Bauman, but when we talk about liquid, flow, and movement, time becomes a vital factor.[2]

> Fluids travel easily. They "flow," "spill," "run out," "splash," "pour over," "leak," "flood," "spray," "drip," "ooze"; unlike solids they are not easily stopped—they pass around some obstacles, dissolve some others and bore and soak their way through others still.[3]

A liquid is unstable, capable of constant movement. Fluidity therefore describes the unsettled nature of a liquid. When we sit in a restaurant it is possible to see the way that a glass of water vibrates slightly with the movement all around it. Tip the glass over, and people at the table quickly jump out of the path of the spreading liquid. As the water hits the floor we can see it make its way, following the contours of the ground or gently soaking into the carpet. Movement and flow are basic to the nature of liquid.

If we are to envisage a liquid church, then movement and change must be part of its basic characteristic. We need to let go of a static model of church that is based primarily on congregation and buildings. In its place we need to develop a notion of Christian community, worship, mission, and organization that is more flexible and responsive to change. The idea of flow is central in this shift in emphasis. Liquid church would work to express itself as a series of movements or flows. As with a liquid, there would be a spreading, oozing, spilling character to these flows.

This does not mean that we should abandon any notion of organization or structure for a liquid church. A liquid will take the shape of any solid container. We are used to the fact that water will assume the shape of the glass in which we serve it. We could take the same water and put it into a different glass, and it will then change to fill that solid shape. The same is true with a flowing liquid. Flow can be controlled in its direction, extent, and shape by solid structures. The heating system in my house relies on the regular flow of hot water around pipes and radiators. A river is similarly affected by the physical environment through which it moves (although over time it also helps to shape that countryside, forming valleys and lakes). The coastline appears to shape the sea, but in reality the sea shapes the coastline. The same will be true of a liquid church. A church that is liquid will be shaped by a series of flows. The flows represent a myriad of moving and changing connections, that is, a kind of network. Liquid church will form a number of different networked connections. These will not only shape its activities but also help us to express the social organization of a liquid church.

NETWORKS AND FLOWS

Networks, according to Manuel Castells, are made up of lines of communication that connect a series of nodes. The nodes represent individuals, organizations, communication systems, or even political structures. Networks produce and are produced by the explosion in communication technologies. This is what constitutes our time, says Castells, as the Informational Age rather than the Industrial Age.[4] Social organization and structure have been decisively affected by the new information revolution. Who holds the power in the network depends on who controls the switches; in this new, fluid environment there are multiple switches, and so power is diffused rather than concentrated.[5] If we want to understand cultural change, then we need to consider the way that networks operate and the way that they have brought this change about. "Networks constitute the new social morphology of our societies, and the diffusion of networking logic substantially modifies the operation and outcomes in processes of production, experience, power, and culture."[6]

Castells illustrates his work by discussing the way that decisions are made in a global economy. He argues that financial systems reside in a process rather than a place, what he calls the "global city." We can't describe the global financial systems by just talking about Wall Street or Frankfurt or London. Communications technology means that all of these sites are linked in millions of different ways. To express the power and effect of the globalization of financial markets we need a broader conception that is based on network connection and processes of decision making, that is, flow. Castells defines this combination of network and flow as the "global city."[7] There is not just one global city connecting financial markets and organizations, says Castells; rather, there are a number. When we look beyond the global city we see other structures that characterize continental, national, and regional economies. All of these also have their nodes of connection to the global network.[8]

The global city is only one example of the many networks that operate in the informational society. Networks are many and varied, and the way that they construct themselves will differ according to the product or service that the network processes. The places where lines of communication connect are described by Castells as nodes. A node may be an organization, a media outlet, a production company, or an individual. Over time some nodes may emerge as being more important than others. These key nodes may arise because of particular historical, geographical, or personal circumstances.[9] The significance of a node will be related to function as well as hierarchy within the network. A company that offers a particular service or product will be connected to various other outlets and customers because it is useful to them. It serves their purposes to be linked. With a growing importance in the network certain sites may become major nodes or hubs where other nodes connect and intersect.

The high speed of communication structures the architecture of the network. The flow of activity and information includes and excludes as it finds its flows through the system. Networks enable a series of flows, and these flows shape contemporary society. "Our society is constructed around flows: flows of capital, flows of information, flows of technology, flows of organizational interaction, flows of images, sounds, and symbols."[10]

Flows are not just to be seen as aspects of social organization; they indicate a series of processes that dominate our social and economic structure.[11] In describing the connections and patterns formed by networks we should not be distracted from the importance of what kind of communication flows between the nodes. The "processes" of communication rather than the structure of the network determine its character. The size or complexity or functioning of the network is of interest, but it does not convey the fact that the real creative power lies with what flows through the network rather than the system.

LIQUID CHURCH: IT'S NOT THAT STRANGE

Making sense of a more fluid or liquid church can seem perplexing. We can find it hard to imagine church where some form of congregational gathering is not at its center. Yet we already have significant aspects of a more fluid and changeable church culture. In the local church and in the wider national and international context there are examples of networks. When we look closely at these networks we can see that they have come about because they enable certain kinds of communication and Christian activity. In other words, we already have a church life that is closely linked to a series of flows or processes. If we are to develop more flexible and fluid church structures, then we should learn from some of the networks that already exist and use these as a pattern for new developments. One result of this will be that we start to realize that a liquid church is not really that threatening or strange. In fact, many of the things we value about our existing church are considerably closer to being fluid rather than solid in character. I have chosen two examples to illustrate how communication and relationship based on networks exist in our solid church environment.

Network Example 1: The Parents and Tots Group

In the village where I live the local church runs a weekly group for young parents and their preschool children—we call them "tots." Around eight to ten women come regularly to the group, and they bring with them preschool children of all ages. The majority of those involved are Christians, although not all of them attend the Anglican church where the group is based. During the morning there is a time for a Bible story and for a song, but most of the time is spent drinking coffee, chatting, and looking after the children. Our church cannot be unusual in running this kind of activity; many churches have similar groups that meet in their buildings. For those who attend, these groups are a source of mutual support, contact, and friendship: the stuff of everyday life. As such they should be regarded as being at the heart of what it means to be church rather than as an activity for just a few that is a good thing but secondary to Sunday worship. This kind of gathering represents a fluid network of communication and relationship. The content of the Bible is flowing into child-sized containers; the love of a Christian community is flowing to and among the women in the group. The understanding that God can meet us everywhere is reinforced.

It is worth reflecting for a moment on how many different connections and lines of communication are represented by what is a relatively small gathering. In the first instance we have the parents and carers who meet and the communication that takes place among them at the group. This is only the tip of the iceberg, for the same people will also meet from time to time throughout the week. If we were to trace the occasions and circumstances where they see each other, we would have a complex web of interactions mapped out. Each of these persons is also connected to her family. A woman may have older children; most of the women have husbands or partners, and they have wider family networks. Each woman is a little hub around which a whole web of connections is maintained. Add to this the contact each of them has with other friends and with the wider community in the village, and the connections begin to multiply again. The church can flow along these networks in the community, bringing the message of Jesus into many and varied life situations.

If we start to think of church as a series of relationship-based connections rather than as a single congregational meeting, then the importance of the parents and tots group becomes clear. In it we have an incredible wealth of complex relational connections, a network that stretches far and wide within the community: a kind of liquid church.

What makes these relationships and connections is not to be found in the particular shape that they develop. Neither do we say this is church because it has an organizational connection to a congregation or a denomination. What makes this church is that people who are connected to Christ are connecting with one another. As they connect with one another they share their fellowship in Christ. As Jesus said, when two or three are gathered together in his name, he is in the midst of them (Matt 18:20). This is what makes such connections church.

Network Example 2: The Worship Song

On a Sunday morning the worship leader strikes up a tune. It's the latest hit worship tune; let's say it was written by the British songwriter Matt Redman from Soul Survivor. Have you ever thought of all the people, organizations, and media activities involved in that song being sung in your church that morning? This is an example of another kind of network that operates in the church as it exists now. The Christian worship scene is an example of Christian global communication. The market for such songs is worldwide, but it has an effect at a local and even an individual level.

We can imagine the various processes of production and communication that have brought the song to us in our church. We can think of Matt sitting at home strumming his guitar and praying that God will touch him once again and help him to write a song. The connections in the network, however, start before the song is written. Matt does not write in a vacuum. He is part of an ongoing ministry, and so he writes in a way that will help in this work. In addition to this he is part of a wider fellowship of Christian musicians and friends who encourage and inspire each other spiritually and musically.

Unless Matt came and taught the song to the worship leader and your church, then a number of relationships and processes were involved in conveying the words and music to your church. The song has been part of a flow of communication that passes through a series of connections. These connections can be complex, and the song might be passed on in a number of different ways. The worship leader at your church may have first heard the song on a CD that was the result of a network of processes and connections such as a recording studio, a record company, and a bookstore or some other commercial outlet. Or the worship leader may have learned the song by hearing it at a Christian event that required a series of other connections, such as the publicity for the event, the organizers of the event, the technical people, the band, and so on. If the worship leader first heard of the song through a music magazine or by coming across it in a worship songbook, another cluster of networked connections would be involved.

How a song gets to us in our service may be an involved and complex process. What this illustrates is that within the Christian community we already have significant communications networks that mirror those in the wider society. So when we sing the latest worship song we participate in a kind of flow that has been made possible by a complex network: liquid church is not really that far away.

WATER ALL AROUND US

The examples illustrate the extent to which, even in a context where solid church predominates, we are already starting to experience a more fluid Christian culture. We can learn a number of lessons from what is happening, and these lessons will guide us toward a more liquid church.

Lesson 1: The Central Importance of Relationships

The parents and tots group shows how existing Christian communities have within them a relational, networked-based dynamic. In many cases these relationships exist alongside the congregation. When we look at what we value about church, more often than not it is these kinds of relationships. Liquid church will take these relational contacts and treat them as the glue that binds the church together. Networked, informal contact between individuals and groups will replace monolithic meetings and formalized friendship.

Lesson 2: The Commodification of Religious Product Enables Flow

The example of the worship song shows how communication processes enliven the act of worship at a local level. The flow of new songs, new ideas about the Christian life, and new approaches to worship makes many of us feel a sense of hope about the church. Our experience of church has ceased to be static in this sense because we feel connected to the ebb and flow of the Spirit around the world. Communication networks and technologies enable this connection between worship groups and individuals to take place. What passes from one individual or one group to another is a well-produced religious product: a commodity.

Liquid church will need to develop commodities that can circulate through networks. This could be a song or a Bible study course or a ministry tape or an event or an art exhibition. The range of possible products is limited only by our imagination and our creative and economic resources.

Lesson 3: Liquid Communication Cannot Be Controlled by Church Leaders

Networks based on informal contact and relationships evolve through natural, organic growth. They cannot be developed or manufactured in the way that many solid churches were managed. The liquid church is more like the Internet, which depends upon the computing power of millions of PCs and the creativity and participation of individuals, companies, and organizations around the world. In a similar way liquid church would have to prioritize the power of individuals and groups to communicate with each other. Through this kind of decentralized growth the church will spread.

Lesson 4: A Liquid Church Will Have Fuzzy Edges

With the parents and tots we see that the network of connections spreads from those inside the church to those who may have no connection with regular Sunday worship. When we start to regard the network itself as church, then the notion of insiders and outsiders starts to break down. Instead, we have a network of communication and relationship where Christian love and mutual support form part of the flow. The boundaries have started to become more fuzzy and less well defined.

Liquid church will see this kind of fuzzy aspect of networks as an advantage. It means that around the church there may grow significant connections to those who have little to do with Christian faith. Through communication these people may become more involved in the various events and activities of the church.

LIQUID NETWORK

Just as congregation is key to solid church, network will be essential for liquid church. Connection to each other and to Christ will be enabled by an emphasis upon communication rather than gathering. The body of Christ will be reenvisioned as a series of dynamic relational contacts. Connection will involve participation where individuals and groups use their spiritual gifts to share the love of Christ with all of those united within the organic, dancing flow of the community. Basic to this connection will be the sharing of products, events, and activities. The commodification of faith will express a contextualized expression of the faith always mindful of the need to be true to Christ. All of this will allow for a more open connection between those who are Christians and those who are seeking a spirituality and meaning in liquid modernity. How we are church, how we communicate, and how we develop an appropriate spirituality will be much more closely related to mission. The fuzzy edges of the network will represent the growing point of the church.

Chapter 5

THE LIQUID DANCE OF GOD

The church is formed and shaped by God. This theological truth must condition the sociological organization of our life together. If we are to adopt a more fluid structure for the Christian community this must be deeply rooted in our understanding of God. Chapter 3 set out a Christology for a liquid church. This chapter returns to the theological discussion by examining the doctrine of God as a basis of the church.

In recent years there has been a renewed interest in the doctrine of God; in particular there has been a growing realization that the life of the people of God is intimately connected to the being of God.[1] God as Father, Son, and Holy Spirit in relationship, Trinity in unity, has been understood as the defining pattern for the church. If liquid church is a realistic option, then not only must it be appropriate in our contemporary culture, but also it must be faithful to our understanding of God. This chapter will locate the idea of a fluid community of God within the contemporary debate concerning the doctrine of the Trinity.

TRINITY: THE LIFE OF THE PEOPLE OF GOD

The origin for much of the current interest in the doctrine of the Trinity has been found in the worship of the church.[2] In worship we encounter a relational God who is Trinity. Worship connects us to the dynamic relationship of the Son to the Father through the Spirit. Christ in his risen humanity is present in the church "in order that he might lift the community into the presence of the Father."[3] At the same time we may say that such worship is possible only because the Holy Spirit makes the people "church" and brings them into the presence of God. James B. Torrance connects the communion of worship to the communion of the Son with the Father, and he uses a phrase from the Nicene Creed that says that Christ was of one being with the Father. In Greek the word that is translated in the Nicene Creed as "of one being" is *homoousios.*

> The patristic phrase "one in being (*homoousios*) with the Father," betokens here that communion with Jesus Christ is communion with God. Therefore to participate by the Spirit in the incarnate Christ's communion with the Father, is to participate in the eternal Son's communion—a relationship which is internal to the Godhead and externally extended to us by grace, established between God and humanity in the incarnation.[4]

God became human in Christ in order that we might be lifted up into the life of the communion of God. The early church father Athanasius expresses this somewhat controversially when he says, "He was made man that we might be made God."[5] This activity of grace in worship, says Torrance, can be understood in two main ways. First it is a movement from God toward humanity. This has a Trinitarian pattern being a movement from the Father, through the Son, and in the Spirit. The second is a movement from humanity toward God, and this too is Trinitarian; to the Father, through the Son, and in the Spirit. The double movement of grace seen in worship, says Torrance, is rooted in the Trinitarian being of God.[6]

Theologians are gradually waking up to the realization that worship has been a key culture carrier for the Christian church. A relational doctrine of the Trinity has been preserved in the tradition and liturgy of many churches, even when it has been largely abandoned as a public theology. By reflecting upon the theology of worship a change in emphasis has started to take place. In the first instance this has affected our approach to understanding who God is, because, as Torrance says, "what God is towards us in worship he is in himself."[7] Second, the doctrine of the Trinity has become a source for a fresh understanding of ethics, the church, and mission. Colin E. Gunton is clear that our understanding of God must affect much more than the worship of the church. He argues that what is revealed in worship should be a pattern for other areas of life.[8] David Cunningham pushes this insight further by arguing that the threeness and oneness of God can be echoed in creation and should affect our understanding of humanity. This has an ethical dimension, says Cunningham, such that the nature of God should affect the way that we live. "Discipleship has something to do with a willingness to allow God to take us up into the divine life, fulfilling the destiny for which we were created."[9] John Zizioulas argues that all of our talk of God should lead us toward a notion of participation or mutual indwelling: "It would be unthinkable to speak of the 'one God' before speaking of the God who is 'communion,' that is to say of the Holy Trinity."[10]

In other words, when we speak of God we speak of the one who is Father, Son, and Holy in communion. The communion of God is essential to his oneness. We do not think of three separate entities who have relationships with each other. Rather, the relationships themselves are part of the being of God.[11] When we come to the communion of the Christian within the body of Christ a similar notion comes into play. The flow of the Spirit, in the words of Zizioulas, "opens our experience for relationship" and communion with Christ.[12] To be one with Christ is to be in communion. As we have seen, this is what Cunningham describes as being taken up into the life of God and Gunton calls being lifted into the presence of the Father.[13] The indwelling of the Christian in the life of God is starting point a doctrine of the church. If liquid church is a theological possibility, then we should be able to encounter it in our reflections upon the life of God. How liquid is the Trinity?

THE LIQUID NATURE OF GOD

Contemporary debates concerning the doctrine of the Trinity have been characterized by a return to the notion of relationship as an organizing metaphor, a move that Cunningham observes has been in response to a dissatisfaction with what has been a more traditional emphasis upon ideas of essence. The claim that God was "a single divine substance" emphasized the notion of a single God. This single being was moreover generally seen as being isolated from the world. This image left little room for expression of an interior relationship within God, that is, Father, Son, and Holy Spirit in communion. It was also difficult to conceive of any kind of relationship between God and creation.[14] Trinitarian theology allows for a greater appreciation of relationship within God and between God and the world. As Robert Jenson puts it:

> The original point of trinitarian dogma and analysis was that God's relations to us are internal to him, and it is carrying out

this insight that the "relation" concept was introduced to define the distinction of identities. If God is "one substance," this is a "substance" with internal relations to other "substances."[15]

The emphasis upon relationships within the One, who is Father, Son, and Holy Spirit, has created a more dynamic understanding God. For a number of theologians this has been expressed in a renewed appreciation of relationship between the being of God and the gospel story. Thus Jürgen Moltmann can suggest that Trinitarian theology should no longer be regarded as a speculative venture. In *The Crucified God* he sets out a vision of the cross as a Trinitarian moment.[16] The death of Jesus involves not only the Son but also the Father and the Holy Spirit in loss and suffering. The Trinity, he suggests, should be seen as "a shorter version of the passion narrative of Christ."[17]

A similar relational emphasis can be seen in the recent work of Paul Fiddes. Fiddes reaches toward a theology of the Trinity that is based on the notion of "three movements of relationship." The movements represent Father, Son, and Holy Spirit.[18] These "persons" of the Trinity should not be regarded as individuals or persons in the modern sense, for, following Augustine, Fiddes suggests that we should focus upon the relations rather than the persons. It is a mistake to imagine that there are persons (in the sense of modern individual) at the end of each relation. This is an impossibility because God is not three but one. Fiddes resolves this problem by suggesting that persons are themselves relations, but they are relations joined in one "event." These ideas find their origin in the Cappadocian fathers of the eastern church, who discuss the triune God as a series of relations among Father, Son, and Holy Spirit. These relations are expressed as begetting or paternity, being begotten or filiation, and being breathed forth or spiration.[19] Fiddes argues that it is impossible to visualize in any clear way three such movements. This is an advantage, because God cannot be objectified like other objects in the world. Rather, thinking of God as relations brings together a theology of "being" with a way of knowing (epistemology).[20]

> The being of God is understood as event and relationship, but only through an epistemology of participation; each only makes sense in the context of the other. We cannot observe, even in our

mind's eye, being which is relationship; it can only be known through the mode of participation.[21]

For Fiddes, participation is the key to understanding the relational nature of God, because participation describes the mutual relationships among Father, Son, and Holy Spirit. It also recognizes the communion between believer and God. Fiddes describes these relationships as *perichoresis*.

PERICHORESIS—THE DANCE OF GOD

Perichoresis, or mutual indwelling or participation, is a Greek word used by the early church fathers to talk about the relationships within the Trinity. The word is not related to *choreia* (from which we get "choreography"), but the similarity, says Fiddes, allows for a play on the two words. In *perichoresis* the dancers do not just intertwine and move around each other, for this is a divine movement. Here we see the persons of the Godhead relating intimately, moving within and through each other in a dance beyond all others.[22]

> So the image of the divine dance is not so much about dancers as about the patterns of the dance itself an interweaving of ecstatic movements. When we speak of parts played by divine persons in perichoresis—for example the Son "indwells" the Father, the Father "contains" the Son, the Spirit "fills" the Father—we are telling a story which enables us to enter the personal currents of love within God.[23]

The dance of God represents a flowing movement of the divine nature. Through the work of the Spirit in and upon the believer, he or she is allowed to participate in this divine life. Fiddes likens this to a kind of "progressive dance." By this he means a dance where the participants move outside of the original circle and invite others to join in the pattern of their movement. So it is also with the divine "story" of the dancers. The divine dance of Father, Son, and Holy Spirit draws us into their energizing and invigorating movement. In our worship and in our mission we participate in the intimate life of God.[24]

TRINITY AND COMMUNITY

The doctrine of the Trinity points to a God who is one and three in movement. The dancing flow of relationship is open-ended, thus drawing us into its current. This is not just a vision for the individual; it is a pattern for the corporate life of the church. Torrance describes *perichoresis* as a twofold relationship between God as Trinity and ourselves through the Holy Spirit. This indwelling is the relationship between humanity and God brought to us in Christ. At the same time it is the relationship between Christ and the church, which allows us to "participate by the Spirit in Jesus' communion with the Father in a life of intimate communion."[25] Gunton describes the church as being a visible "echo" of "the dynamic relations between the three persons who together constitute the deity." The church in this sense is called to be the reality of the eternal God at a finite level. The being of the church should be grounded in a God who is "the source of the being of all things, the eternal energies of the three persons of the Trinity as they are in perichoretic interrelation."[26]

To echo the life of God, the church will of necessity be driven away from self-importance and toward what Gunton calls "the creative and recreative presence of God to the world."[27] These creative and re-creative activities are seen in the proclamation of the gospel and in the celebration of the sacraments, all of which means that the church does not exist as a timeless institution. Rather, says Gunton, the church exists only where the Spirit connects people to Christ and links them together into a community.[28]

Cunningham has a similar vision for the being of God as a source of community in contemporary society. The doctrine of the Trinity, he suggests, is a challenge to individualism. In place of what he calls "the modern cult of the individual, it teaches us to think in terms of complex webs of mutuality and participation."[29]

Liquid Trinity

Theologically the nature of the church is linked to the being of God. If God is seen as a flow of relationships among Father, Son, and Holy Spirit, then we find here a significant boost to a more fluid kind of church. The idea of mission and worship as the Trinitarian dance of God is growing in popularity and significance within theological circles. Such an idea is empowering and inspirational in that it allows for the participation of believers in the intimacy of God's fellowship. Worship and mission are linked by a mystical theology based on this intimacy. The vision of a church as networks of relationship and communication suddenly takes on a powerful symbolic significance in the light of these ideas. The static monolith of the congregation is replaced by a dynamic, inclusive, and fluid dance of intimate communication. In this sense liquid church does not just reflect the life of God. It joins in with that life and it is indwelt by that life: liquid God and liquid church.

Chapter 6

SHAPING THE LIQUID CHURCH

A network-based liquid church cannot be planned. It must grow. People who are looking for God will connect to the network because it offers what they want. In this sense liquid church locates itself firmly in the consumer nature of society. It seeks to offer the reality and fullness of God in a form that people want. There is no sellout involved, no dumbing down of the message. In fact, liquid church will remain committed to an exacting orthodoxy and a committed theology. The next four chapters show how liquid church can adapt to a consumer culture while remaining deeply rooted in theological frameworks. The starting point for this discussion will be the realization within the sociology of religion that belief and believing are undergoing significant changes in liquid modernity. The British comedian Stephen Fry recently lamented the changes in British culture, and he quoted G. K. Chesterton, who said, "The problem is that when people stop believing in God, they start to believe in anything."[1]

There has been a religious sea change in contemporary society. In most Western countries the Christian church has experienced significant decline. At the same time belief and believing appear to be ever-increasing phenomena.[2] Robert Wuthnow sums up this change of mood in the much-used phrase "I am spiritual, but I am not religious."[3] What people mean by this is that they might have religious or spiritual experiences, but they are not regular churchgoers. Spirituality in this sense is more aspirational; it encompasses a wide range of beliefs and practices, some of which may be Christian but many of which may not. Most people have rejected solid church either as refuge or as club, and in its place, as Fry points out, they have started to believe just about anything. Liquid church is not just a way to connect with contemporary changes in spirituality; it is also the logical extension of many of the changes that have characterized religious life over the last fifty or so years. As solid church has tried to adapt to modernity, it has adopted ways of using contemporary media and communications to package faith and offer it in the marketplace. Liquid church takes some of these changes and pushes them further by taking account of a more fluid market.

Believing without Belonging

Liquid church takes as its starting point the change in Western religious life, a change that Grace Davie describes as "believing without belonging."[4] In her study of religion in Britain since 1945 she observes that most people appear to express their religious preferences by staying away from church rather than by attending. At the same time, remarkably few people have turned away from belief by adopting atheism or abandoning spirituality.[5] There is a similar phenomenon in the United States. Wuthnow argues that this could be described as a shift from a spirituality of "dwelling" to what he calls a spirituality of "seeking."[6] The spirituality of dwelling finds its natural place in settled, domestic communities. The spirituality of seeking, he says, is more suited to times of change and uncertainty. Part of the reason for this is that the experience of most people has changed considerably in the last forty years or so. This change represents a shift from a relatively unchanging and secure environment to one of constant change. The result is that people's lives lack the previous securities.

> At one time people were residents of their communities; now they are commuters. Thus images of stable dwellings have increasingly been replaced by images of those who have left home: the migrant worker, the exile, the refugee, the drifter, the person who feels alienated or displaced, the person lost in the cosmos, the traveling salesman, the lonesome net surfer, the lonely face in the crowd, the marginal person, the vagrant, the dispossessed or homeless person.[7]

Alongside these changes in employment and social existence Wuthnow observes a similar spiritual change. Whereas once people expressed their faith through membership in religious organizations, now they do so through a pursuit of connections. Believers search through various organizations, disciplines, and practices and yet may never feel a sense of belonging. This rootless existence is paralleled, he says, by a similar shift in working practices. Whereas once work was located in brick-and-mortar factories, now it is more likely to be located in information technologies and communication. In a similar way faith was once located in churches and synagogues, but now it is more akin to what he calls "information flows." Seeker spirituality is characterized by a series of ideas and beliefs, and these are promulgated by a varied collection of therapists, gurus, and spiritual guides.[8] What we have then is a new spiritual marketplace with a vast array of beliefs and practices for sale. To understand this environment and its dynamics we need to examine consumer culture more closely.

Shopping for a Liquid Church

Shopping characterizes all of contemporary life. Individuals, says Zygmunt Bauman, constantly compare prices, casting their eyes along the shelves, feeling the goods, and assessing the balance on their credit cards. "Whatever we do and whatever name we attach to our activity it is a kind of shopping, or an activity shaped in the likeness of shopping. The code in which our 'life policy' is scripted is derived from the pragmatics of shopping."[9]

The culture of shopping arises from the numbers of products to choose from. The multiplication of choice produces a competitive arena, not just for those selling the products but also for the consumer. Life becomes a series of choices. Some may be good and some may be bad, but we can be sure that we will be judged by others on the suitability of our purchases. Consumer society is like a race where the finishing line is moving faster than the runners. Each of us is cast in a sea of choices where what is at stake is our ability to be competent, to make the right choice. Consuming therefore becomes a fluid environment where we never come to the end or reach our goal. Instead of an eventual finishing point, all that we have is the addictive behavior of seeking the right choices.[10]

When theologians or preachers discuss our consumer society, they often aim at what they see as materialism. By this they mean that people focus on things rather than on spiritual matters. Some of us are obsessed with things, but at the same time many people would argue that consuming goes beyond the acquisition of a stylish carpet or a fancy car. In the new shopping environment the product is only half the story.

Consumption, says Jean Baudrillard, should never be treated just as the satisfaction of "needs." If we want to understand the meaning that things have for us, then we have to go behind the "thing itself" to ask what this product signifies.[11] An example could be a car. It doesn't take too much imagination to see that a car signifies more than just a means of getting from A to B. Cars are status symbols, and they make sense in a system of similar symbols. If we get some idea of the way that the car acts as a symbol in our society, then we will get a better idea of what it means to consume. This perspective is echoed by Mike Featherstone: "There is the question of the emotional pleasures of consumption, the dreams and desires which become celebrated in consumer cultural imagery and particular sites of consumption which variously generate direct bodily excitement and aesthetic pleasures."[12] Our competency as a shopper is challenged not so much by the choice of products, events, and experiences but by what they represent: the hopes and dreams, the aspirations and pleasures. To shop is to seek for something beyond ourselves. To reduce this to materialism is to miss the point, or more importantly it is to miss an opportunity. For this "reaching beyond ourselves" indicates a spiritual inclination in many of the everyday activities of shopping. Rather than condemn the shopper as materialist, liquid church would take shopping seriously as a spiritual exercise.

THE SPIRITUALITY OF THE SHOPPER

James B. Twitchell is critical of cultural commentators who eschew the value of advertising and consumption. He argues that the problem is not that we are materialist but that we are not materialist enough![13]

> If we craved objects and knew what they meant, there would be no need to add meaning through advertising. We would just gather, use, toss out, or hoard indiscriminately. But we don't. First, we don't know what to gather and, second, we like to trade what we have gathered. Third, we need to know how to value objects that have little practical use. What is clear is that most things in and of themselves do not mean enough. In fact, what we crave may not be objects at all but their meaning.[14]

Consumption is not primarily a materialist occupation, and here Twitchell echoes Baudrillard; in fact, it is based on the exchange and enjoyment of "meanings." The role of advertising is to add value to objects by investing them with meaning. In this sense, says Twitchell, advertising performs a role in our society that historically has been associated with religion. In the past value was located with God in the world beyond. In contemporary society value has been relocated in material goods and their use.[15] Twitchell uses the term adcult to describe this religious dimension of advertising. Advertising is like religion, he says, in that it is part of a meaning-making process. Religion and advertising attempt to build a bridge across the gap between ourselves and things, and they do this by offering a systematic order.[16]

The meaning of things is related to our place in society and the world. The clothes I wear, the car I drive, the music I listen too all locate me in relation to my friends and neighbors. Consumer choice is related to the development of taste. In this sense taste represents an ordered system for choosing between various products. Taste, according to Pierre Bourdieu, is related to a system of social boundaries, which he calls distinctions. Consumer choice links us to some people and separates us from others.[17] Consumption is therefore about finding who we are in the world. Twitchell interprets this as a promise of salvation. The meaning making of advertising, he says, offers the possibility of redemption.[18] Nor is Twitchell alone in this insight; David Lyon also speaks of consumption in similar terms, as being a kind of salvation.[19]

> Consumerism has become central to the social and cultural life of the technologically advanced societies in the later twentieth century. Meaning is sought as a "redemptive gospel" in consumption. And cultural identities are formed through processes of selective consumption.[20]

Clearly more is in play than we may have first thought when we visit the shopping mall or when we flick through the pages of a magazine. Christian leaders are right to see consumption as a challenge to belief, but they are wrong to locate this in the material world of the object. If Twitchell and others are right, then adcult represents an alternative source of meaning to the traditional Christian gospel. This means that as we shop we search for a kind of salvation.

THE ALL-CONSUMING CHURCH

Solid church has often criticized consumption, but this criticism has not prevented contemporary worshipers from generating a Christian sensibility that is built upon consuming spirituality. When Christians move to a new town they shop around for a church. This kind of behavior is common. Most of us will have some kind of wish list in this situation: good preaching, warm fellowship, exciting youth ministry. These factors are on our list of products we look for in a possible church. Churches in the UK and in the US recognize that this is a major factor in their success. Most lively churches aim to be attractive to people who might be visiting, so we see the emergence of various strategies for welcoming outsiders. An example of this is the growing popularity of the Welcome Team who are there to get our names, sign us up for a pastoral visit, and generally make us feel a part of what is going on. Most of those drifting into church in this way will already be believers, but we all appreciate the effort put into this kind of activity.

Solid church has grown most successfully from attracting those who are already Christians, and not just those who have newly moved into the area. Many of our biggest churches have quietly grown by adding to their number people who join them from other churches in their town or city. The reasons are fairly obvious. Christians have started to shop around for the church that offers the best package. There are many reasons for this. We may become dissatisfied with the level of service in our regular church. Perhaps a new minister takes over the congregation, and suddenly the church is under new management and what's offered is no longer to our liking. Maybe it is that the goods seem a bit outdated: less than fresh worship, clergy who have hung around too long on the shelf. Then we hear of exciting new things happening at a church near by, and we go and check it out. This is Christian consuming, the spirituality of the shopper, and it is alive and well in our churches.

The idea that churches compete in a spiritual marketplace was an early idea of Peter Berger. According to Berger, contemporary society would bring about fundamental changes in the way that churches operated. Competition, for believers, would create a more aggressive environment for religious groups. This new competitive context means that we may even see take-over bids and mergers where churches combine in order to maximize their effectiveness in the market.[21] Thus the ecumenical movement or the church planting movement could be interpreted within the economic model as related to market share and competition. Reginald Bibby describes churches in Canada as offering an "a la carte" menu of choice, and he talks about "religious suppliers" experiencing problems with the creation of "product" and "product distribution."[22] All of this means that the culture of contemporary churches has emerged as a strategy for survival in the marketplace. Solid church is a successful form of marketing.

THE SPIRITUAL MARKETPLACE

In *Selling God*[23] Laurence Moore argues that the contemporary discussion concerning the secularization of religion should be supplemented by the notion of what he calls "the commodification of religion." Since the nineteenth century churches in the United States, he says, have grown because they have found ways to exploit and influence the marketplace. Through a variety of activities religion has become one of a number of self-improving and "cultured" leisure activities that individuals buy.[24] At first religious leaders entered the marketplace to censor and condemn.

> However, the work of religious leaders and moralists in the market-place of culture was immediately entangled in a related but distinguishable enterprise. Rather than remaining aloof, they entered their own inventive contributions into the market. Initially these were restricted to the market of reading material, but their cultural production diversified. Religious leaders even sponsored "non-profit" organizations with moral and reform goals that competed with the appeal of popular entertainments. By degrees religion took on the shape of a commodity.[25]

By competing in a marketplace of diversions and "entertainments," religion was to be transformed into a product. Moore's argument creates links between the shape of contemporary religion in the US and the modern consumer society. This link between the marketplace and churches is gathering support from a number of different cultural historians.[26] From this perspective the religious opposition to consumption can be seen less as a prophetic or spiritual challenge and more as the tactics of a competitor.

If we adopt this view, then it becomes clear that from about the eighteenth century religious institutions have been competing with the leisure industry for people's time and attention (and money). The result has been that in order to compete, churches have reshaped faith as an attraction or a commodity. If this argument is true, then shopping for a church makes perfect sense, and spiritual consumers are what most churches have set out to produce. A good example of this is the success of the Alpha course in the UK and worldwide. Alpha has managed to harness contemporary advertising and communication techniques to develop an easy-to-use evangelism course for local churches. The success of the course is due in part to its ability to offer those who seek the meaning of life an opportunity to hear more in a nonthreatening environment. Stephan Hunt links the franchised logo and advertising of Alpha to what he calls the "just looking tradition." He argues that Alpha appeals to people drawn by the opportunity for increased knowledge and personal growth.[27] A similar approach to evangelism can be seen in the spreading influence of churches such as Willow Creek Community Church.

Like Alpha, Willow Creek sets out to offer the Christian faith in a way that connects with contemporary culture. The church identifies with the notion of "seekers" and has developed a style of communication and church life that takes account of this spirituality. Consequently religious language in worship and in preaching has been restructured around the perceived needs and cultural assumptions of those who are, as yet, outside of the church. This is the seeker-sensitive church that has developed its own style of "Seeker Services."[28] In a religious marketplace Willow Creek sets out to give customers what they want. As the church tries to make itself more accessible to a wider public, it reforms itself.

The work of Moore and others is important because it focuses attention on the changes in contemporary religious life. From their analyses it is possible to see how market processes and patterns of production and consumption have shaped the Christian church. Far from rejecting such developments as superficial or theologically problematic, I believe that the commodification is essential for evangelism. A good example would be the What Would Jesus Do craze that swept

through youth groups and churches a few years ago. WWJD
was a hyped marketing opportunity that made some people
a lot of money. But at the same time it was one of the few
things that contextualized Christian faith in the fast-moving,
symbolic, fashion-conscious world of early adolescence. The
WWJD bracelets existed as fashion statement in playgrounds
and classrooms in a way that evangelists, Christian worship
bands, or anything else in the Christian subculture has singu-
larly failed to do. The reason is that for many of these younger
teenagers identity is uniquely invested in the purchase and
display of products. These products act as symbols within a
wider meaning system. WWJD managed to incarnate Christ
inside this fairly arid world, and it did so by commodification.

LIQUID CHURCH—THE NEXT STEP IN THE RELIGIOUS MARKETPLACE

From what has been said so far it can be argued that even
within solid church a number of developments are starting to
take account of a new consumer culture. These changes are
extremely important because they are a sign that solid church
may find ways to adapt to the new context. Those seeking a
club or refuge will still need these kinds of services marketed
to them in the most professional way possible.

At the same time it would be a mistake to assume that
because of these developments there is no need for any new
thinking in our churches, for as we have seen, many people are
seeking a spirituality. The problem for solid church is that its
one-size-fits-all environment is adapted only for one or two
kinds of spiritual consumers. The need to keep the congregation happy, the club members active, and those who are seeking refuge safe, means that solid church is unable to maneuver
in this fluid environment. What is needed is a more flexible
church, one that is able to respond to the changing needs of
people. The challenge for the liquid church is how it can do
this without losing its theological heart.

Chapter 7

REGULATING THE FLOW, PART ONE: THE WORD OF GOD

If liquid church embraces the believer as a consumer, does this mean that whatever the customer wants is acceptable? Is a market-related church inevitably a sellout of the gospel and ultimately of God? These questions are extremely important and need a serious answer. Solid church, for all its faults, is a relatively predictable environment. If we abandon our safety, what guarantees are there that we will not find ourselves sinking rather than going with the flow?

The first thing to say is that in and of itself there are no guarantees. If we are to find our way in the new, fluid environment, then we will need to make some basic decision about what we will take as a guide. The theology and values of the church are not up for grabs. A liquid church must be committed to Christ and the gospel in order to be church. This does not mean that we go into this situation with a completed blueprint of what we expect to see in our new church or that we have already decided how and in what exact terms we will express the message of Christ. What this means is that we have a clear sense of our theological priorities and limits. One way of expressing this is to take an analogy from sports.

A tennis court is made up of a series of lines, and across the middle there is a net. To play tennis involves following a number of fairly simple rules. These include rules such as the ball must bounce within the lines, each player must hit the ball with single stroke, and the ball can bounce on each side of the net only once. Given a tennis ball, a couple of rackets, and a court with a net, it is possible to play any number of different games. It is also possible to start to play tennis but to cheat or adapt the rules as you go along. So the players might agree that the ball can bounce twice or that on the serve it can land anywhere in the court, and so on. All of these are possible and may

be enjoyable, but when you alter the rules you cease to play
tennis and start to play something else. This does not mean
that within the basic rules of tennis the players may not express themselves and improvise. If you compare the play of
people such as Andre Agassi, Pete Sampras, or Tim Henman it
is obvious that different approaches to the game and styles of
play are not only possible; they make the game great. The
same is true of the Christian church.

Before we embark on a new pattern for church life we need
to set down a few markers that define what we think are the
limits of the game. These markers carry weight only because
we choose to allow them to limit our play. Yet in laying out the
area of play and the basic rules I have had an eye upon the historical tradition of the church and the weight of theological
discussion concerning the church. This discussion is in two
parts. In this chapter we discuss the limits of a liquid church in
relation to the doctrine of the Word of God. In chapter 9 we
take up this subject of limits again and deal with the work of
the Holy Spirit and the theology of grace.

THE MARKS OF THE TRUE CHURCH

At the time of the Reformation the previous certainties
of the Catholic Church were being overthrown. If the new
churches were to break away from the unified body of the historic church, then how were the Reformers to assure themselves and their followers that these were true churches? The
solution was to relocate the "truth" of the church in the communication of the gospel. If the gospel was truly communicated, then there was the church.

In 1552 the Reformers of the English church published
what they called The Articles of Religion. In all there are thirty-
nine articles, and they contain a series of doctrinal, ecclesiastical, and ethical rulings that were designed to form the basis
for the new Anglican Church. Article 19 is entitled "Of the
Church," and it set out the definition of the church. The text
(in *The Book of Common Prayer*) reads:

> The visible Church of Christ is a congregation of faithful men, in
> the which the pure Word of God is preached, and the Sacraments
> duly ministered according to Christ's ordinance in all those things
> that of necessity are requisite of the same.

The exclusively male language represents the expression of the day, but the message is clear. The church is not a building or a place or an organization of clergy. It is a group of people. The word *congregation* refers to all of those in the country who are faithful to Christ and also the local gathering. The important thing, from our point of view, is that what makes the gathering (of whatever type) the true church is not its social organization but the Word of God. The emphasis is therefore upon the authentic communication of the Word and the sacraments. In this formula the English Reformers were influenced by the Reformation in Geneva and the work of John Calvin.

In his *Institutes of the Christian Religion* Calvin sets out what he regards as the defining marks of the church. His terminology is similar to that of *The Book of Common Prayer.* For Calvin the visible church is made up of true believers and those who are not. The true believers in this sense may be seen as a kind of invisible church.[1] This assumption of ambiguity in the church also extends in Calvin's thinking to whole congregations or a whole church such as the Catholic Church, which may in one way or another be in error.[2] The marks of church are there to enable us to make a judgment as to what is a church and what is not.[3]

> From this the face of the church comes forth and becomes visible to our eyes. Wherever we see the Word of God purely preached and heard, and the sacraments administered according to Christ's institution, there, it is not to be doubted, a church of God exists. For his promise cannot fail: "Wherever two or three are gathered in my name, there I am in the midst of them."[4]

THE FLOW OF WORD AND SACRAMENT

In developing a more fluid notion of church it is essential that we do not float away into a world of our own imagining. These traditional formulations were developed in a similar period of change and renewal in the church. They indicate an important safeguard that will offer some helpful rules of play for our creativity and innovation.

Liquid church is to be based upon a series of evolving and changing networks. Through these networks there will be a flow of communication. If we are to develop a true church, then we would be mistaken if we concentrated upon the construction of the network. The shape of the network or even its membership is less important than what flows through it. This is where these formulations from Calvin and the Anglican Church are helpful, because they point toward the importance of a right communication of Christ. This should be our central concern. How can Christ be communicated, or to put this in more relational terms, how can the network facilitate communion with Christ and the dance of the Holy Trinity? Here Karl Barth's theology has something to say.

Although Barth was Swiss, he began his theological work in prewar Germany. During the 1930s he was associated with those within the German church who opposed the political philosophy of the ruling Nazi party. In 1935 he was expelled from his teaching post at the University of Bonn and returned to Switzerland.[5] Barth's monumental work, *The Church Dogmatics*, was written to identify how we might be assured that the distinctive talk of the church about God is truly the Word of God.[6] Barth's concern is to develop a theological system that helps the church to review its talk about God. He calls this process of review and correction "dogmatics."[7] The purpose of dogmatics is to enable the church to be more faithful in the task of proclaiming the Word of God. Barth's work therefore offers a starting point for considering how we might judge the truth of a liquid church.

TESTING THE WATERS

Like Calvin, Barth identifies the mark of the true church as being the right preaching of the gospel and the right administration of the sacraments.[8]

That the church claims to be preaching the Word of God should not mislead us, says Barth. The proclamation of the church "is and always will be man's word."[9] At the same time these human words make a claim to be God's Word. What the church says, however, is not necessarily or inevitably God's Word. Through God's action it becomes "proclamation."

> Proclamation and the Church are, of course, simply and visibly there just as the bread and wine of communion are simply and visibly there and the distributing, eating and drinking of the bread and wine in Communion take place simply and visibly. They are not simply and visibly there, however, as they want to

be and should be, as theologically relevant entities, as realities of
revelation and faith. They have ever and again to come into
being as this.[10]

The event of the revelation of the Word of God makes proclamation real proclamation. We can see the bread and the
wine, and we can hear the words of the sermon, but what
makes them real and genuine as revelation can come only
from God. For Barth this is an event that is ever to be repeated
and can never be assured or predicted.[11]

Although it cannot "predict" the revelation of God in its
talk, the church is still called to proclaim. Talking about God is
human activity conditioned by history and context, and it is
necessarily so. As Barth says, "Talk about God becomes in
every age specific and distinctive talk."[12] The wonder is that
this specific talk may become the occasion for the revelation
of the Word of God.

While clearly prioritizing the preaching and sacraments of
the church, Barth acknowledges that the church talks about
God on a number of occasions. He specifically mentions the
education of young people as an example, and he also dis-
cusses the extent to which social work can be thought of as
"talk about God." Alongside preaching Barth also touches on
hymnology and the liturgy of the church. These too he says are
proclamation, and as such they should be subject to theological scrutiny. He observes that when hymn books are revised,
theologians are rarely consulted, and as he rather ruefully puts
it, "The results naturally correspond."[13]

He also allows, but in a much qualified way, that God may
speak through those who are outside of the church.[14]

Yet in all of these places the same issue is at stake. When
and to what extent can these various expressions be seen as
the true proclamation of the Word of God? The task of dogmatics is to develop a critical culture within the church that can
help the church to reflect upon its talk about God however it
may take place.

If liquid church is to be true church, then it also needs to
take these issues seriously. In doing so it may be possible to
keep faith with the spirit of Barth while acknowledging a wider
range of communications as being the churches' talk about
God. The various activities of the contemporary church may
not have been envisaged by Barth, but to the extent that we

regard these as talk about God they become places where we hope that God will be revealed. Theological discussion of these types of communication is essential. To do this there must be some agreed theological commitments for those involved. This is where some notion of an overarching Christian story is important.

HOLDING ON TO THE CHRISTIAN STORY

In *Telling the Story* Andrew Walker describes the gospel as "The Grand Narrative" of the Christian people.[15] He argues that although the Christian gospel has been told many times over and in a great many different ways, with different emphases and so on, it is still possible to set out in a few short paragraphs the basic pattern of this story. He then offers his summary of The Grand Narrative, which is an elaboration on the historic creeds of the church.[16]

> Historically, the gospel as a grand narrative was predicated—not overnight, but over a protracted period of history and experience—upon a number of interlinked Old and New Testament narrations. This also included both the ordering of the narrations, the theological reflection upon them by the apostles, Fathers, and doctors of the early Church. [17]

Walker's point is that this story identifies the Christian people; it is our story. We need to continually retell it, and as we do so we give it a different expression, but at its most basic the story remains the same. Among cultures and different churches we see a variety of emphases, but still the story in its basic components remains familiar. Walker's summary of the Grand Narrative starts with the existence of God outside time and the world, then moves to a description of the creation of humanity of God's image, then the fall. This leads to an account of God's dealing with the Jews and in the life of Christ. Jesus as God's revelation and redemption in his life, death, resurrection, and ascension forms the heart of the narrative. From Christ emerges the church as his gathered disciples following his way; the church bears the good news of Jesus. Finally all things are brought to their conclusion, and all things are brought together in the eternal life of God.[18]

Walker's notion of a Grand Narrative of the Christian people is a little more accessible than the many volumes of

Barth's *Church Dogmatics*, but it can be said to operate in roughly the same way that Barth suggests theology should do in the church. Those individuals and groups that make up the networks of a liquid church need to set their limits by embracing an orthodoxy rooted in the creeds and tradition of the church. In a fluid environment where church life becomes a series of communications and relationships within an ever-changing network, the idea of the story of the people of God connects the liquid church to its theological roots. A commitment to orthodoxy provides assurance in the midst of the flow. Within the network at various times individuals and groups can use the commitment to a core theology to assess the content of what is communicated, and this core theology can become a source for new expression and reformulation of the activities of the church. Some people may act as theologians in the way that Barth imagines. Within the network there may be those whose calling is to help to evaluate and assess the liquid church in terms of the commitment to historic Christianity.

THE WORD OF GOD AND THE LIQUID CHURCH

In all of this the primary commitment of the church should to communicate the good news of Christ. The message of the Reformers and of Barth indicates that purity in the church is never guaranteed by institutional arrangements. The church is truly itself when it communicates Christ. This therefore must be the emphasis of the liquid church. The intention throughout should be that the content of the network flow of the church should be Christ.

Like all other churches, liquid church cannot guarantee that this will be the case. All that we can do is to express our theological commitments clearly and then be willing to review what emerges in the light of these rules of play. This does not sound particularly watertight, but solid church is in many ways not different. What theological checks and balances operate in the average congregation? In many ways liquid church acts in a similar manner to regular church. The difference is that it will need to take communication and commodification more seriously as aspects of the flow within networks. By paying attention to what is communicated, we can seek to remain faithful to the dynamic and living Word of God.

Chapter 8

DESIRE FOR GOD

Liquid church involves a radical change in attitude for the church. Church leaders will need a fundamental change of heart if they are to start to take consumer culture seriously. Instead of opposing materialism and treating consumer choice as evil, we need to begin to embrace the sensibilities of consumption. This means that we must develop a church life that connects with what people want, and one vital ingredient will make this change possible. The church must change its emphasis from meeting people's spiritual needs to stimulating their desires. Solid church is set up to convince people of their need of God and then deliver salvation in response to this need. Liquid church replaces need with desire.

NEED TO DESIRE

Need has been at the heart of developments in contemporary society. Tony Walter points out that the idea of need has become ingrained in the disciplines of psychology, self-help movements, and therapy courses. Need, he says, is so all-pervasive that we have ceased to regard it negatively.[1] "People today assume that needs are not bad things to be eliminated, but good things to be met."[2] Walter identifies the way that churches have embraced the language of need. In this new environment God has become someone who "meets our needs."[3]

Solid church has located itself as the arbiter of such needs. Many are the church programs that have been developed to "meet the needs of the local community." Evangelism has taken as its starting point the assumption that people have a need for God. Solid church has found a place for itself in world by setting out to meet people's need of God. Need in this sense has been prescribed and anticipated; it is related to a paternalistic authority that knows best. Need is limited, boundaried, part of a common human condition that can be met and satisfied.

Spiritual need is taught and policed in heavy church. By contrast, a fluid culture is not based on the reasonable limits and prescribed notions of need. In liquid modernity the relationship between need and the consumer has moved on. Shopping, as we have seen, has less to do with the acquiring material things and more to do with the consumption of the added meaning associated with products.[4] This shift is basic to the new, fluid environment. Consumption is no longer about meeting basic material requirements of life. Instead, it has become something much more central to our sense of self. Shopping is not about need but about desire.[5]

Desire, not need, drives our choice in the supermarket and in the shopping mall. We desire the images, associations, and status that have been linked to various products. Shopping is therefore an activity that is to some extent driven by a search for something that is beyond ourselves. Desire, according to Zygmunt Bauman, is more "ephemeral, evasive and capricious" than need.[6]

Desire cannot be satisfied or met in the same way that can be said for need. Desire remains with us, pushing us to search after the next best thing. In this sense desire is nonreferential, because we are unable to locate its true end or its fulfillment.

Solid church has found a comfortable role for itself in developing a gospel based on spiritual need. Such need can be predicted and policed. Those who are unaware must be convinced of their need and then offered the requisite solution. Need has allowed ministers and religious professionals to appear to be still in control of their churches. The problem is that for most of us life is no longer run according to need. Something drives us that is less predictable and much more passionate: desire. In the mall and in the church, desire increasingly motivates our actions and generates our choice. If church is to embrace a more fluid path, then it needs to come to terms with the opportunities and the limitations of desire.

DESIRE FOR GOD

A liquid church would be built around the realization that people seek encounter with God. Spiritual hunger, desire, and pleasure are just below the surface. If we think for a moment about the little things that people buy to decorate their homes— candles, incense burners, pictures, and so on—behind many of these objects there can be observed a spiritual dimension. The current trend toward gardening is also evidence of not only aesthetic but also spiritual sensibilities. Contemplation, quietude, meditation, and an appreciation of the restorative qualities of beauty and nature are among the reasons why people spend time in their gardens. Similar observations could be made about much of the music that we buy or the movies we go to, for in these too we can see aspects of a spiritual quest.

Spiritual desire is evident in so many areas of life, and a huge industry has grown up in response to this desire. Much of this can be characterized as part of the New Age movement. "New Age" obviously covers a range of activities and beliefs, but taken as a whole it is evidence that millions of people are searching for spiritual experience. Paul Heelas acknowledges the diversity of New Age practice and belief, but he argues for the existence of common themes that he describes as "self spirituality." This kind of spirituality "explains why life—as conventionally experienced—is not what it should be; it provides an account of what it is to find perfection; and it provides the means for obtaining salvation."[7]

These are obviously spiritual concerns that concern significant numbers of people in contemporary society. The response of solid church to the New Age has been predictably negative. Most church ministers see the New Age as misguided at best and demonic at worst. This is not the place to go into a detailed discussion of the theological and moral implications of various New Age beliefs; the point here is much more focused and simple. First, the various activities associated with the New Age demonstrate a vast ocean of desire for spiritual encounter. Second, what is equally clear is that solid church is at sea in this new environment.

The church has spent its time trying to convince people that they need God, while these same people busily seek spiritual experience. The big question is why so few people see solid church as a place where they might find what they are looking for. This question takes us to the heart of the need for a more fluid Christian faith. When people say that they are "spiritual but not religious" they identify themselves with a desire for God, but they do not see the need to search for this within institutional religion. The reason for this by and large is that solid church has created an exclusive club out of Christian believing. In backing the desire of some people for safety and refuge, solid church has created communities where spiritual experience comes at a cost of membership and belonging to a whole bunch of institutional and community activities. The spiritual seeker sees the price tag attached to faith and looks for satisfaction elsewhere. Alongside this it needs to be said that some seekers find the challenge of Christian believing to be too costly in terms of ethics or personal morality. A great deal is made of this by some Christians who see New Age spirituality as lacking an ethical challenge and thus seems a "softer option" than Christian faith. Yet once we get inside our churches we realize that such ethical niceties and rigor are not quite what they seem from our rhetoric. In terms of moral and ethical choices, many Christians live lives that are very similar to those of people outside of the church.[8]

LIQUID EVANGELISM

We move from liquid church as an imaginary concept to liquid church as a reality by working with two simple assertions:

1. Everyone has spiritual desire.

2. Church should be designed around people's desire for God.

Our consumer culture is based on a search for meaning. At its heart this search is spiritual, and as such, it represents a search for something beyond ourselves. Liquid church begins by affirming this search as the place to start in sharing faith and in building a new kind of church life. It is worth dwelling on this for a moment. Solid church has tended to build its sense of identity from the widespread rejection of its creed and community life by the rest of society. The refuge feels all the more cozy if the rest of the world is against it. I suggest that we dump this mindset and instead assume that people are already hungry for God. This doesn't mean that they are knocking on our doors desperate to get in, but it does mean that we take serious notice of the way people are starting to live their lives. In particular we recognize that in all sorts of different and varied ways they already express a desire for God.

If people want God, then the problem doesn't lie with those outside the church; it rests on those inside. We have got things seriously wrong, as an analogy about fishing will show. Imagine that the church is in a fishing boat. We are surrounded by water that is stocked with hungry fish. We see inexperienced people fishing with unsuitable equipment but nonetheless doing extremely well. Yet we have been all day without a bite. The church is sitting in communities where significant numbers of people are spiritually hungry. Yet even in this situation we are unable to attract them into our meetings. We have great buildings and excellent patterns of worship, which are like the boats and the ways of fishing. Perhaps even more infuriating is the fact that in Christ we have the way, the truth, and the life, the genuine gospel, and yet we still can't get people to take the bait. In contrast to the church, people with fewer resources, less developed patterns of belief, and not as much respect in the community—in other words, the poorly equipped fishing boats—are overwhelmed by the people being drawn into their activities. In such circumstances most people look at what they are doing and try and work out what is wrong with their approach to catching fish. What can they learn from their low-tech rivals? The church, however, is so proud of its flashy boats and huge nets that it has failed to learn the lessons.

If we want to learn how to fish, we need to truly believe that people want God. The fish rise to the bait; they are feeding. So liquid church would reshape itself around worshipers as consumers. Spiritual life would recognize that shopping is the natural way of interaction with all aspects of life, including the spiritual. A fluid church would abandon congregational structures in favor of a varied and changing diet of worship, prayer, study, and activity. The assumption that what we offer in our morning service may be boring or unpalatable but ultimately is good for you will be challenged. In its place will be a responsive, flexible pattern of church life that seeks to deliver not only what individuals want but also what draws on the depth and variety of the Christian tradition. Such a consumer-oriented church would be likely avoid the dumbing down of the "middle path," "we must not offend," "we need to carry the congregation with us" mentality of heavy church. Instead, a variety of spiritual expressions drawing on the riches of a number of Christian traditions would be available.

INTEGRITY AND CHOICE IN THE LIQUID CHURCH

Choice must be basic to the new shape of church. Choice, however, does not mean that we accept that the customer is always right. Liquid church must seek a high level of authenticity in its spirituality and integrity in its allegiance to Christ. In being more true to the faith than we perceive solid church to be we will find the resources to connect with the spiritual aspiration and energies of contemporary culture. The belief that drives this move is simple: people want a real and profound experience of God. Solid church has made the mistake of underestimating the desire for an authentic spiritual expression. In an attempt to connect with people and be relevant it has played down some of the more challenging and extreme aspects of the Christian life. Liquid church would try to reverse this process. The emphasis upon choice would be fostered by exploring the variety and depth of Christian spirituality, worship, and missionary service.

An example of choice would be the development of a varied pattern of prayer within a community. In a building or a church, different rooms might be given over to different forms of prayer; these rooms could be seen as part of a School for Prayer. Through courses and workshops, individuals and groups could come to this kind of spirituality center and explore faith within and among different traditions. Space within the building could be given to different ways of praying. Space for spiritual directors or personal prayer trainers could be created. A room for praying with icons, maybe another for praying through the creative arts, worship prayer, and movement could be explored elsewhere. Aromatherapy and prayer with essential oils might also play a part. Instead of a regular worship time there could be special events, performances, and exhibitions that help people to develop these practices further.

Such a center would enable those within the faith and those who might be drawn to it to explore the contours of the faith. By digging deeper into our tradition we will find the resources to develop ways of living the Christian life that will stretch us beyond the rather humdrum existence of congregational life. In all of this we must remain focused on the life of God, which gives us our energy and renews us from without and from within. God who is Father, Son, and Holy Spirit remains the origin and end point for our worship and our engagement with the world. The customer is not always right, but in many cases we can give the customer what he or she wants by being more truly ourselves.

Chapter 9

REGULATING THE FLOW, PART TWO: THE SPIRIT AND GRACE

Liquid church will find its energy and it creativity in the widespread search for spirituality and meaning in popular culture. Yet there remain some important theological questions; not least of these is how we understand the working of God in a consumerist environment and what limits there are to his activity. Not all networked markets based on consumer choice are good; the illegal trade in drugs is an obvious example. But given our assumption that all people want to search for spirituality, we must search for a framework in which the church can meet the market need.

In chapter 7 we explored the limits of liquid church in terms of a theological commitment to Christian orthodoxy. The argument for a series of commitments or rules was related to the communication of the Word of God in the church. In this chapter we return to the question of the theological framework for a liquid church and now focus upon the doctrine of the Holy Spirit and the theology of grace. Jürgen Moltmann's theology of the work of the Holy Spirit as "the spirit of life" helps us understand how God might be at work in popular spirituality. These insights are compared with the theology of special and common grace developed by Abraham Kuyper. Finally we will look at ways of distinguishing between religious experiences by discussing the ideas of Jonathan Edwards.

THE SPIRIT OF LIFE

Moltmann argues that we need to take the informal experiences of people seriously as an arena where the Spirit of God may be at work. If we contain God within the church or if we suggest that the Spirit is able to work only through a particular kind of preaching, then we limit God.[1]

> . . . the continual assertion that God's Spirit is bound to the church, its word and sacraments, its authority, its institutions and ministries impoverishes the congregations. It empties the churches, while the Spirit emigrates to the spontaneous groups and personal experience.[2]

Moltmann indicates that an experience of the Spirit within the believer has increasingly become the key factor in spirituality, and such experiences are not limited to church. This means that we need to develop a theology of the Spirit that can take account of the work of God outside of the workings of the institution of the church. It also needs to recognize that God is at work beyond the Christian community and even beyond the activities of individual believers. If we make this move and cease to regard God as being limited by the church, then we need to adopt a theology that embraces the activity of God in the world. Moltmann identifies the doctrine of the Holy Spirit as the key to this change in our thinking.

His starting point is to identify the link between the Spirit of God and life: "the spirit of life." While many people may never have experienced charismatic spirituality or any kind of specifically Christian experience of God, most have a consciousness of the "spirit of life." This spirit, says Moltmann, is seen in "the love of life which delights us, and the energies of the spirit are the living energies which the love of life awakens in us."[3]

When we look at the Holy Spirit we see the energy of God that creates and sustains life. These two, the spirit of life and the Holy Spirit, must be related. This means that when we talk about the experience of life, the Holy Spirit cannot be separated from this; rather, we should see it as being integral to all that makes life a living and vibrant experience. "The Spirit sets this life in the presence of the living God and in the great river of eternal love."[4]

In order to connect the Holy Spirit with the general flow of life, Moltmann adopts the term "The Spirit of Life." In *The Trinity and the Kingdom of God*[5] he gives what he calls "appropriate independence" to the Father, who is the Creator of all being, and the Holy Spirit, who is the "living energy of life."[6] The result of this, he says, is that when we connect with the Spirit we sense an awareness of God, "with and beneath the experience of life, which gives us assurance of God's fellowship and love."[7]

This awareness is not limited to formal church gatherings or to those who are already committed Christians. The Spirit of God responds to people's search and touches them with an experience of the presence and love of God.

The Spirit of Life as discussed by Moltmann allows for a sense that God is active in people who may be far from church and that his activity is vibrant and essential. If liquid church is to embrace consumption as a form of life, then we can see how God might be a part of this, but only to the extent that what is being pursued is life or life-giving. Sometimes people desire what is not life-giving; in fact, it may be the opposite. Moltmann's understanding of the Holy Spirit as the power of God that brings life is helpful in this sense because it allows us to critically embrace a consumerist society by making distinctions between what leads to life and what does not. This, however, still leaves a further question: How do we make a distinction between the life-sustaining and enriching activity of the Spirit of Life and the salvific activity of God? In short, what is the relationship between life and eternal life?

This question is crucial for liquid church, because we will need to embrace the consuming desires of people, but we need to do this without naïveté. Life is sinful, and people get things wrong. Moreover, significant aspects of life are good, but they do not necessarily lead to salvation in Christ. A good example is sports. As an activity and as an entertainment sports have many undeniably good qualities, but does football really lead us to God? When we feel alive and energized when our team wins the match, is this the same as an encounter with God? If we take Moltmann's notion of the Spirit of Life uncritically, then we might be led in this direction and find ourselves outside of a theological commitment to the Grand Narrative of the people of God. Thus when we embrace what Moltmann suggests we must do so in a discriminating way. One way to do this is to suggest that God's activity in the world, grace, might be described in different ways. This is where Abraham Kuyper's distinction between common and special grace is helpful.

COMMON AND SPECIAL GRACE

Kuyper's starting point is with the Calvinist doctrine of the sovereignty of God. If God is sovereign, he argues, then God's lordship must extend over all of life. To restrict the rule of God to within the building of the church or to an exclusively Christian circle of influence is to deny that God is Lord. Moreover, says Kuyper, it is important to affirm that Christ is at work inside and outside the church to avoid a dualistic approach to life where God is concerned only with the soul.[8]

> This way of thinking results in your living in two distinct circles of thought: in the very circumscribed circle of your soul's salvation on the one hand, and in the spacious, life encompassing sphere of the world on the other. Your Christ is at home in the former but not the latter. From that opposition and false proportionality springs all narrow-mindedness, all inner unreality, if not all sanctimoniousness and powerlessness.[9]

To avoid these problems we need to conceive of a way that God works in the church and in the wider world.[10] Kuyper's solution is to posit that God's grace works in two kinds of ways: common grace and saving or special grace.[11]

Common grace is the work of God that sustains creation and holds back the tide of the lethal effects of the fall of humanity.[12] Without common grace, says Kuyper, a cursed creation would cease to exist. Common grace creates an open space of possibility in which history is allowed to develop and exist.[13] All of human history is in the hands of God, and he is involved with every move toward progress and development, including those in science, education, the arts, and technology.[14]

Common grace is an account of God's work in all of creation, but it is not special or saving in that it is not a particular work of God for an individual. Saving grace refers to the work of re-creation, and this is a special work of God. Special grace goes beyond restraining the effects of the fall that common grace does; special grace creates new things.[15] "The saved person is a new creature in Christ, he is a new human being."[16]

Like the individual, the church should be seen as a new creation of God. These two are re-created. This involves the redemption of what was created. In physical and cultural terms this new, re-created community shares a good many characteristics with the society and culture around it. At the same time what has been re-created, says Kuyper, cannot be explained from creation. What has emerged has not come from what was originally created, neither can it be fully explained by what went before. This means that, according to

Kuyper, between creation and re-creation there is a significant discontinuity that comes from the work of Christ.

Kuyper, writing in 1884, made this distinction partly to encourage the Christian people of his day to reach beyond the confines of the church toward an involvement in society. His theology is helpful because it allows us to distinguish between how we evaluate human culture and the work of God in that culture. Kuyper's use of common grace operates much like Moltmann's concept of Spirit of Life to encourage Christians to consider a wider framework of life and to see these areas of life as valuable to God and part of the theological worldview. The distinction between an order of creation and that of re-creation is also helpful, because it preserves the salvific nature of the work of God. It enables us to keep in mind that even though God is at work in the area of the arts, it will not always be for the purpose of evangelism. For the liquid church this is important, because it allows for cultural engagement without always reducing the activity to an evangelistic opportunity. To identify that there is an act of recreation as well as creation, special grace as well as common grace, encourages us to make sure that both areas form part of the work of any church.

THE RELIGIOUS AFFECTIONS

If we left this discussion at this point we would be in serious danger of accepting all religious experience and searching as being blessed by the Spirit of God. There would therefore be no real need for a church of any kind and little need for the idea of being incorporated into Christ. It is important, therefore, to get a right balance between affirming the spiritual desire of people and their concern for religious experience and the concept that not all religious inclinations and experiences are of equal worth. This matter has been discussed at some length by Jonathan Edwards.

In *The Religious Affections,* which was first published in 1746, Edwards reflects on the tidal wave of revival that spread through New England and brought with it all manner of religious expression and experience. Edwards uses the term *affection* for those things to which we are inclined and the intense experience that results when we encounter them.[17]

Edwards prioritizes religious affections in the Christian faith.

> . . . for who will deny that true religion consists in a great measure in vigorous and lively actings of the inclination and will of the soul, or the fervent exercises of the heart. That religion which God requires, and will accept, does not consist in weak, dull and life-less wishes, raising us but a little above the state of indifference: God, in His word, greatly insists upon it that we be in good earnest, "fervent in Spirit," and our heart vigorously engaged in religion.[18]

If the Christian religion consists "in great part" of religious affections, how then should we discern right affections from wrong ones?[19]

The problem is that the grace of God can be "very small" and hard to discern. To be too quick in deciding what is of God and what is not is to run the risk of considerable arrogance.[20] It is also the case that individuals through lack of experience or through their weakness to sin may not be able to see where God is at work.[21] This kind of caution leads Edwards to identify a number of experiences as being neither a sign of God's gracious activity nor a sign that God is not active. Included in these ob-servations are a number of physical and religious experiences. An example of this is given in relation to particular effects upon the body. Edwards makes it clear that affections of all kinds, not just those that arise from the saving work of Christ,[22] will have a bodily result. So it cannot be read from the intensity of bodily experiences whether these are of God or not. At the same time, because the experience of God is profound we should not be surprised at seeing people groaning or panting in the Spirit. But such activity does not guarantee or ensure that God is at work. In some situations the Spirit of God may influence people, but this may not be an influence of a "saving nature."[23] Edwards identifies this activity of the Spirit of God as "common." Com-mon grace is distinct from special or saving grace.

> Not all those persons who are subject to any kind of influence of the Spirit of God are ordinarily called spiritual in the New Testa-ment. They who have only the common influences of God's Spirit are not so called, in places above, but only those who have the special, gracious and saving influences of God's Spirit.[24]

The Spirit of God is in people and in creation, but this is different from the saving work of God, says Edwards, and even those who have experience of God's Spirit may resist. As Edwards puts it, "The un-mortified corruption of the heart may quench the Spirit of God.[25]

When it comes to religious affections that are an act of God's gracious activity, Edwards sets out a number of theological criteria that will be present if they are held to be true. These include the realization that these affections come from God and therefore will conform to his nature and that the affections will be directed toward the worship of the true God as revealed in Jesus Christ.[26]

The effect of this theological pattern, combined with a cautious humility and common sense, is that Edwards creates a framework for understanding religious experience that welcomes ambiguity without embracing all experience uncritically as a sign of the work of God.

Edwards offers a number of insights that are pertinent to the development of a liquid church. The first is that it is possible to allow for God to be at work in the religious desires of contemporary consumers. We may never know what exactly the status of this activity may be. What we do know, however, is that the general or common work of God indicates that God's Spirit is at work in the spiritual desires and experiences of those currently outside the church. These experiences can be valued as a work of God, but they may not be a "saving or special grace." As such they do, however, indicate a place from which evangelism may grow. Here God is already at work for the common good. If God is at work, perhaps we should embrace what he is doing. Not all religious experience will be of God; not all spiritual longing will lead to God. But this does not mean that we may not be able to connect with what is happening in the wider culture with a new kind of consumer-oriented church.

THE SPIRIT, GRACE, AND THE AFFECTIONS

With Moltmann's suggestion that we should regard the Holy Spirit as the Spirit of Life we see how the dance of God can start to connect not just to human culture but to creation as a whole. Very few of us believe that God is confined to our churches, but we may have prayed and acted as if this were the case. Edwards's theology offers a note of caution to that of Moltmann: We must not be tempted to assume that everything that affirms life necessarily implies that God's Spirit is at work as saving grace.

In a consumer culture we must be able to embrace fluidity and a certain amount of chaos while remaining firmly committed to the gospel of God. To do this we need Barth and Moltmann, and Kuyper and Edwards to provide us with frameworks to help us in this process. Kuyper offers a social or cultural appreciation of the workings of grace. His distinction between common and special grace is significant in that it can help us to be at work with the Spirit in life and also to engage in the communication of Christ toward eternal life. The problem with this distinction, however, is that in practice we are rarely able to make this distinction. In this ambiguity many evangelicals have abandoned the wider social engagement and declared that they will work solely in the area of special or saving grace. In liquid modernity such a tactic is no longer appropriate (if it ever was). Liquid church must accept that a fluid and networked communion with God is fuzzy and hard to define. When you get close, the work of God in creation and salvation is jumbled together. This is where Edwards is useful.

Edwards is able to identify a series of experiences and religious behaviors that are neither good nor necessarily bad. He encourages us to embrace ambiguity in spirituality. Faced with the turmoil of religious revival, he offers a few helpful guidelines. In most cases, he says, we don't know if God is at work toward salvation or if he is not. As a result liquid church should start by affirming what can be seen as positive in the contemporary spiritual quest. God may be at work in surprising ways. We can give voice to this affirmation by way of the idea of common grace. This idea allows us to embrace these affections as positive and possibly of God, but they do not have to be regarded as special or salvific. Liquid church must prioritize special grace and remain focused on the work of God's Spirit toward salvation. The communication of Christ within the network of the church should be characterized by the distinctive work of the Holy Spirit for salvation. The spirituality of popular culture is a starting point, but from this a more specific work of the Spirit must develop. Edwards gives us a language for this, but he also cautions us that we may not be able to tell what kind of work of God is which. This means that the communication of Christ and work of the Spirit within liquid church will be ambiguous. We may not know exactly where it is that wind blows. We may not know where it comes from or where it goes to. If liquid church is to survive in a consumer society, then it will need to embrace the ambiguity of the work of God, but it must do this while remaining committed to a vision of the saving work of Christ, special grace. Edwards gives us a perspective within which we can start to negotiate our way in this complicated and fluid environment.

Chapter 10

INSIDE THE LIQUID CHURCH

So far the argument has mainly been at a theoretical level. In terms of sociology and theology the possibility of a more fluid church has been explored. If liquid church is to be a reality, then it will involve a practical expression of a different kind of church. While it is clear that some aspects of contemporary church life might be seen as more liquid, a liquid church at this point is something of a dream. Describing any kind of dream can be an inexact pastime, and dreams about church in particular can be very difficult to get right. That said, in this final chapter I will set out in as much detail as I can a number of characteristics of liquid church as I imagine it to be. For those involved in solid church, this chapter may indicate ways in which a more liquid way of being the Christian community could start to emerge. I must warn that my descriptions are not watertight plans designed to be put into action throughout Christendom. There will be many different and creative ways of being a liquid church, and these are my incomplete and barely glimpsed dreams of a different kind of church. At best they say, it *could* be like this.

DREAM ONE: THE NETWORK

Liquid church would replace congregation with communication. The networked church would connect individuals, groups, and organizations in series of flows. Connection would gather around hubs and would be made up of connecting nodes. A hub might be a retreat center, a sports team, a music group, a record company, a Christian shop, and so on. Connection to individuals and groups would involve sharing the life of God in a variety of ways. An example might be a joining together of those in the network to work for social justice. Through Internet connection, email communication, or personal contact and localized gatherings, such an action could be planned and then completed. Another example of the way a network might operate could be in the use of Bible-study material. Material produced either by individuals or by a Christian company can be gradually spread through the networks. Once again it might be possible to use the Internet, or one person could give material to another person.

One idea might be to foster relationship and connection through a variety of reading groups. These sorts of meetings already take place, but more emphasis could be placed on them as the way that church can be refocused in informal, relational connections. Some of those in the network will see their role primarily in terms of the production of events or products. We already have Christian companies that publish books, CDs, and so on. This kind of production needs to be supplemented by what I call productive hubs, that is, creative producers who are able to develop materials and activities that connect locally. Leadership in the liquid church will need to evolve to include songwriters and video makers and event organizers. These people will be at the heart of many of the hubs.

Individual nodes represent the connection of believers or those with no belief to the communication flow of the network. Membership is no longer measured by attendance at worship. Instead, it is assessed in terms of participation in the network. Much like a website can evaluate its significance in terms of number of hits, liquid church will be based on participation: how many people participate in the activities of the network.

DREAM TWO: COMMUNITY

Community in liquid modernity is in a state of continual change. This can be problematic for individuals, and as a result commentators can become pessimistic and proclaim that community is dead. In my view this is mistaken. Community has not died, but it has changed. People still want to be with each other, they still want to feel that they have significant relationships, and they still want to make a difference in other people's lives. In liquid modernity this desire is expressed through constant communication.

One example of this is the use of cell phones, which make it possible for us to communicate with friends and relatives while we are on the move. The result of this is that a culture of continual contact has started to evolve. The ability to use the pager facility to send text messages from phone to phone at a fraction of the cost of a call has meant that millions of young people in Europe have developed a new form of connectivity. The average young person in the UK sends and receives dozens of these messages a day. This is community, but it is community based on communication rather than gathering. This is not, however, a virtual community. The people sending the messages know each other and regularly see each other face to face. The messages are a way of enjoying connection with one another.

Christian community needs to adopt this and similar kinds of communication as its measure of fellowship in Christ. Meetings are of less significance than the quality and kind of communication that takes place in the church. Small-group meetings and interest-group meetings will be a part of a liquid church. So, for example, a group meeting to share an interest in religious art or the ethics of business may be one of the ways that people connect. But the communication within the group should be supplemented by frequent communication that could include using technology such as cell phones, text messaging, and email.

DREAM THREE: COMMUNITIES OF CHOICE

Liquid church will abandon congregational structures in favor of a varied and changing diet of worship, prayer, study, and activity. It will challenge the assumption that what is offered in the morning service is good for you, even though it may be boring or unpalatable. It will present a responsive, flexible pattern of church life that seeks to deliver what individuals want and also draws on the depth and variety of the Christian tradition.

Relationship and communication would follow choice. Thus community would evolve around what people find interesting, attractive, or compelling. A good example would be a spirituality based on the environment. Liquid church might begin to explore the idea of prayer walks or spiritual journeys. Groups might begin to find ways to connect prayer life to walking activities. It might be possible to take people on activities that combine meditation and mountain climbing.

Another, less athletic idea might be a guided stroll along a river or a stream with places to stop, pray, and read the Bible.

A potential criticism of churches as a self-selecting group is that such a group will be less socially diverse than the regular kind of church. But most churches are already fairly limited in the kinds of people they gather. Communities based around choice could bring a wide diversity together precisely because they are based on shared interest. An example of this would be the variety of people who have children of the same age in a preschool class. Another example would be the different kinds of people who follow a football team. Yet, however they are organized, these kinds of communities would prioritize informal relationships. Connections would be based upon a natural affiliation rather than on a sense of obligation or monolithic gathering. A similar connection is seen in the way that groups may gather around an act of service in a local community, for example, a welfare program for the homeless or a pressure group working for justice for those detained in prisons around the world. These groups connect people because they offer a common place for the investment in voluntary activity. The hope would be that intimacy of Christian fellowship would restore a qualitative character to the life of the church, offering genuine connection and relationship rather than what so often feels like a pretense of community.

DREAM FOUR: LEADERSHIP FROM EXAMPLE

Whereas the heavy church ordains those who are safe and steady and willing to hold the fort, in the liquid church leadership will no longer be able to rely on appointment and authority. When worshipers are free to shop, they will gravitate toward those they perceive as being enlightened and in the know, and these people will emerge as the leaders. Those who are perceived to have met with God, been in his presence, and found themselves to be changed by his Spirit, will be the guides, the teachers who lead by the example of their holiness, discipline, and passion. The priorities of the worship consumer are different; he or she seeks those who are saintly, inspired, and full of the Spirit of God.

Those who desire God will be willing to follow these kinds of leaders along the demanding paths of spiritual discipline. Liquid church will replace norms and routines with clearly expressed ways of living in the presence of God. The spiritual path may be presented as an exacting and testing way for followers of Jesus. Leaders relocate themselves as fellow travelers telling tales of wondrous sights and risky pathways. The way of the cross of Jesus will be seen to involve committed engagement and some suffering. To live in the grace and energizing of the Spirit will arise from the exercise of submission and repentance. These gospel perspectives will be shared by those who are seen as examples rather than taught by those who assume authority based on outside appointment.

The lowest common denominator of congregational life will be replaced by the pursuit of the holy. This corresponds to Zygmunt Bauman's discussion of the difference between health and fitness. Health is located in solid modernity and is based on conforming to basic norms, rules, and standardized expectations. Fitness in contrast is an openness to the unexpected—a readiness for what life may throw at you.[1]

Liquid church will have more akin to fitness than health. An example of this is the growth in the retreat movement. In the US and in the UK the numbers of people going on retreats at monasteries and other religious communities has increased over the last few years. One of the reasons for this is that Christian people seek more committed and extreme spiritualities than those they are fed week by week in the pew. Liquid church would look for ways to develop and expand this evident interest in spiritualities of depth.

Another example of the way that congregational leaders are being supplemented by those who are seen as being spiritually experienced or trained is the growth in spiritual direction. Spiritual directors are people who have trained to guide others in their prayer life. The numbers of people who meet with spiritual directors to talk about their prayer life has steadily risen. Here again we see that people are already searching for a spirituality that goes beyond the safe norms of the congregation. The comfortable lifestyle of heavy church is being supplemented by more demanding spiritual routines and exercises. The religious in convents and monasteries are sought out as holy examples and guides. In addition to this many parish clergy are retraining as spiritual directors, because they too yearn for a deeper spirituality. Liquid church would find ways to set these people free to explore church as an expression of this desire for a deeper spiritual path and ministry.

DREAM FIVE: EVENTS AND IMAGINATION

Solid church offers worship as a regular and regulated weekly diet. Liquid church will need to adopt a more attractive and imaginative approach to events and activities. An example of this is an event that was recently held in London. To celebrate the millennium the National Gallery in London held an exhibition. The event was called "Seeing Salvation," and it focused on religious art, in particular representations of Jesus from the earliest Christian period until the present day. The exhibition was a huge success—it was one of the most visited exhibitions at the National Gallery that year. To complement the event at the gallery, a documentary series was shown on BBC television.

The exhibition was well presented, and several of the pieces were powerful. Interestingly, however, looking through the catalogue it was clear that nearly all of the pictures and sculptures in the show had come from various galleries and museums around London or from within the UK. Unlike many other shows, this one did not rely upon that "wow" factor of seeing something that has never been seen before in the UK. Most of the items were drawn from the National Gallery's permanent collection and could have been viewed at any time by a discerning viewer who was willing to wander around a few rooms and hop between the centuries.

The interesting question is why people flocked in the thousands to see these pieces in this exhibition. The answer must be related to the way that the National Gallery was able to take what was already on show in various places around the country and bring it together into an attractive package. Suddenly a few religious paintings and sculptures had become and event with a poster, a television show, and a catchy name, "Seeing Salvation." What seems most interesting is the way that the gallery found a way to get people to come and look at the pictures by re-presenting them in a new way. It's worth noting that there was no hint of dumbing down or popularizing at this exhibition. These were serious pieces of art on show in the premier gallery in central London. In the catalogue and in the documentary series, the theological nature of these works of art was made plain. The viewer was left in no doubt these were religious works designed to move us to faith. There was no apology for this or even any attempt to explain away the faith aspect of the exhibition; it was presented as the way things were. What made this material accessible was that it had been put together in a new way.

The church has a good deal in common with an institution such as the National Gallery. We too have a significant cultural heritage of music, literature, art, and spiritual expression. We also might be seen as perhaps a little stuffy and maybe at times out of touch or highbrow. The glories of the Christian church, like the pictures in any major art gallery, have been constantly on show and in the public gaze for generations. Our regular church services are a little like the public rooms in the National Gallery. Our wares are on show free to be viewed by the public, but on the whole most people stay away. What we need to learn to do is re-present the faith in ways that touch the imagination and fire the interest of the general public.

An example of how we might reimagine the church came to me when I visited the local gym. There on the notice board was a simple poster offering a fitness check-up. For those of us who have fallen out of a regular sport and exercise routine, this is a way back in to a more healthy lifestyle. Of course, the swimming pool, gym, and soccer fields have been there for years. What the fitness check offers is a chance to start again on this kind of activity. This got me thinking about the way we offer spiritual growth and renewal in the church. Maybe we should be developing ways back in to the habit of meeting with God on regular basis. A spiritual check-up with a per- sonal counselor may be an interesting way to go! The problem with solid church is that it would turn this kind of idea into a routine, so it would suggest that everyone joining the church must have a check-up. Liquid church would see that the short term and an offer for a limited period only will be attractive and catch the eye of the discerning consumer. Keeping the run of an event short is an essential part of making it special. This is particularly the case when we are dealing with the press. The culture of media-based publicity relies upon what is new. The regular habits of solid church don't cause any great stir in the press.

Liquid church will need to adopt a regular cycle of new releases, events, and product launches. Of course not all new things are new. A good many media events are a celebration of what is old. The thirtieth year of a Broadway show, for instance, becomes the reason for a makeover and relaunch. The anniversary of the death of a classical composer results in a rerelease of his music in a boxed CD set. Liquid church needs to present spiritual events and products in a similar form. In the liquid world the failure to produce a new product line eventually leads to death.

DREAM SIX: WORSHIP IN A LIQUID CHURCH

Worship is essential for any church, but as we have seen this could be in small groups or in much larger citywide festivals as well as in medium-sized congregations. But how can a liquid church offer worship without reproducing the problems of solid church? In this dream I set out in some detail some examples of what I call decentered worship, or worship that does not rely upon a congregational dynamic. Three quite different worship experiences have led me to feel that such imagining may be possible. The first is a contemporary example drawn from an experimental act of worship held during Lent 2000 in St. Paul's Cathedral in London. The second is based on a description of worship in a medieval church before the Reformation in England. The third is based on experience of midday prayers in an Orthodox church on the island of Tinos in Greece. Finally, I describe a worship event I helped to plan at Greenbelt Festival.

The St. Paul's Labyrinth

The labyrinth in St. Paul's Cathedral was organized by several informal worship groups based in London. It was made from a series of white lines on a carpet. The lines formed an intricate pathway along which people could walk. This kind of walkway was inspired by the labyrinth that can be found on the floor of the cathedral in Chartres, France. The Chartres labyrinth is an intricate walkway laid out in tiles on the floor of the nave of this ancient cathedral. In medieval times pilgrims to the cathedral would walk or crawl around the labyrinth as a spiritual exercise.[2] For the worshiper in the Middle Ages, the labyrinth may have represented a symbolic journey, possibly to the Holy Land.

In the St. Paul's labyrinth the symbolic journey was combined with a series of prayer stations. At various points on the walkway areas were set aside with activities for reflection, meditation, and prayer. Each worshiper was given a personal CD player on which there was accompanying music and a spoken meditative guide to the activities within the labyrinth. The prayer stations involved a number of different activities. One station had a bucket with water in it. Worshipers were invited to reflect on aspects of their life that they felt were less than perfect, sins committed, and wrongs experienced. Then they were asked to drop a small pebble into the bucket of water, as a sign of turning these experiences over to God. At another station there was a laptop computer. On the computer screen a number of images of candles were on display. By hitting the space bar on the computer it was possible to light one of these candles. The worshipers were invited to think for a time of a friend in need or a situation in the world. In the quiet they were asked to pray for what they had been thinking about and to light a candle on the screen to represent their prayer. The journey around the labyrinth could take from thirty minutes to an hour depending on the time spent at each station. Several people could walk the path at the same time, thus sharing a communal experience that also allows for considerable individual prayer and spirituality.

Worship before the English Reformation

Church worship has not always been congregational in the way that we experience it. In the fifteenth and early sixteenth century, immediately before the Reformation in England, a visit to the local church could be a much more decentered experience than we might imagine. Eamon Duffy describes how during this period receiving the communion was often limited to Easter only.[3]

Although people ate the host only annually, they were very often to be found in church "hearing the mass." The focus of such church attendance was the moment when the priest raised the host above their above their head. This was known as sacring. For the worshiper seeing the holy bread lifted in this manner was a considerable blessing. In many churches in England at this time as well as a central main altar there would be a series of chapels around the outside of the church, each with its own altar. Mass would be said simultaneously on several of these altars by a large number of priests. Duffy describes how these services would be carefully timed so that the worshiper could see the sacred host elevated more than one time by the clergy at the various altars. A bell would be rung at each altar as the host was raised so that worshipers could catch a glimpse of it at this special moment.[4]

What Duffy describes is an experience of worship quite unlike the contemporary idea of congregational participation. The multiple nature of the altars means that being a participant in the service may mean a number of different things. Many people would come to church and engage in a series of private prayers, turning their attention to the activities at the central or side altars only as the bell was rung. Something about this notion of private and corporate spirituality is very contemporary in its appeal. This kind of experience has a good deal in common with some aspects of Orthodox worship.

Greek Orthodox Worship

On a recent holiday my family and I made a brief visit to an Orthodox church on a small Greek island. The church was a center of pilgrimage, and many of those making their way to midday prayer did so on their hands and knees. Inside the church a variety of activities was offered. Worshipers could kiss the sacred icon, light candles, eat the blessed bread that was available, fill small bottles with holy oil, and wander around the church—this offered the possibility of more icon kissing. The service was conducted while all of this took place. As the singing and chanting continued the priest read petitions quietly in front of the altar. At one side of the church people were writing prayers on small pieces of paper, and these prayers eventually found their way to the priest. Worshipers were therefore able to participate in a varied and individual way. This was a corporate moment, but it was also decentered. The static and largely passive congregation that is characteristic of solid church seemed a million miles away. Those attending the service appeared to do what ever they liked. A few stood and listened to the prayers, but most were engaged in one or more of the activities.

Decentered Worship at Greenbelt

Inspired by the St. Paul's labyrinth and the Orthodox service in Greece, I have tried to develop my style of liquid worship. One such service was prepared for a worship time at the UK-based arts and worship event, Greenbelt Festival. The service was designed around the idea of the face of God. Around the room we placed a number of different activity centers, each drawing on a different aspect of the theme. These included a picture of Christ and some candles that could be lit. There was a photocopier, and people were invited to make a copy of their face (taking care to close their eyes!). These pictures were then displayed during the worship. There was also a large mirror, and written on it were the words "And all of us, with unveiled faces, seeing the glory of the Lord as though reflected in a mirror, are being transformed into the same image from one degree of glory to another" (2 Cor 3:18).

When people arrived, they were shown the various activities, and then for around one hour we sang worship songs. People were free to sing the songs, pray quietly, or wander around the room and take part in the activities. This was again an attempt to get away from the congregational style of corporate worship that is characteristic of solid church. The worship was most appreciated by many children who came to the event. They found the possibility of activity liberating, yet they could do this while others were involved in deep, meditative prayer.

The Orthodox style of worship, and to some extent the labyrinth, represent premodern spiritualities and traditions. As such they perhaps represent a glimpse beyond the heavy, congregation-orientated life of many of our churches. In these examples the relationship to tradition, identity, spiritual discipline, and practice has been reorientated in ways that differ significantly from our solid social structures, and as such they indicate a way forward to a more liquid church. It might be possible to take our congregationally designed buildings and re-create them as imaginative and creative space where people explore a variety of worship practices. This kind of decentered spiritual space need not necessarily be always used for some kind of a worship service. The labyrinth is interesting in this connection because it offers a way of experiencing a deep encounter with God in an individualized but also communal experience. One way that this could be used might be as part of a café that could use the labyrinth to offer a place for spiritual exploration and experience as well as pastries and cappuccinos.

THE WAY FORWARD FOR LIQUID CHURCH

In this final chapter I have tried to offer some clues as to the way that a liquid church might develop. These dreams are only that at present. They will come to life only if church leaders and individual Christians want to take them up and bring them to life. This is much easier than it might first appear. In the first instance most of us are already part of several networks of relationship and communication. These networks exist because we want them to; they work for us. The next stage is to expand these connections by developing particular ways of meeting, products that can be circulated, and events that can provide a focus for communication. In all of this the priority must be upon relational connection rather than events or meetings. The products we develop are there to stimulate connection rather than the other way around.

The quality of relationships must connect to a spirituality that is rooted in our participation in Christ. Networked church must be connected to Christ. This is a mystical and spiritual reality that is based on the working of the Holy Spirit touching us and renewing us. Liquid church is not a program or a mission project; it is a community rooted in the fellowship of the Holy Trinity. The intimate dance of God can be experienced only by those who accept the invitation.

NOTES

NOTES TO INTRODUCTION

1. P. J. Hefner, "Ninth Locus: The Church," in *Christian Dogmatics*, ed. Carl E. Braaten and Robert W. Jenson (Philadelphia: Fortress, 1984), 2:191.

2. Ibid., 19.

3. Paul Tillich, quoted in Hefner, "Ninth Locus," 2:199.

4. G. W. Bromiley, *Theological Dictionary of the New Testament,* ed. Gerhard Kittel and Gerhard Friedrich (Exeter: Paternoster, 1985), 397.

5. J. D. G. Dunn, *The Theology of Paul the Apostle* (Edinburgh: T&T Clark; Grand Rapids, Mich.: Eerdmans, 1998), 539.

6. Ibid., 538.

7. Ibid., 541.

8. Ibid.

9. Ibid., 542.

10. Alfred Loisy, quoted in Hans Küng, *The Church* (London: Search Press, 1968), 43.

11. See the bibliography in G. E. Ladd, *A Theology of the New Testament* (London: Lutterworth, 1974).

12. Ibid., 111.

13. Ibid., 113.

14. Küng, *The Church,* 65.

15. Ibid., 64.

NOTES TO CHAPTER 1

1. Jon Pahl, *Youth Ministry in Modern America 1930—Present* (Peabody, Mass.: Hendrickson, 2000), 56–72; J. Raybury III, *Dance, Children, Dance* (Wheaton, Ill.: Tyndale House Publishers, 1984); Joel A. Carpenter, *Revive Us Again: The Reawakening of American Fundamentalism* (Oxford: Oxford University Press, 1997), 161–76; and Douglas L. Johnson, *Contending for the*

Faith: A History of the Evangelical Movement in the Universities and Colleges (Leicester: Inter-Varsity, 1979).

2. See Grace Davie, *Religion in Britain Since 1945: Believing Without Belonging,* Making Contemporary Britain (Oxford: Blackwell, 1994); and William K. Kay and Leslie J. Francis, *Drift from the Churches: Attitude Toward Christianity During Childhood and Adolescence* (Cardiff: University of Wales Press, 1996).

3. David Lyon, *Jesus in Disneyland: Religion in Postmodern Times* (Cambridge, UK; Malden, Mass.: Polity Press, 2000), 76.

4. Ulrich Beck, *Risk Society: Toward a New Modernity* (trans. Mark Ritter; London: Sage, 1992), 12.

5. Manuel Castells, *The Rise of the Network Society* (2d ed.; Oxford: Blackwell, 2000), 1–4.

6. Leonard I. Sweet, *Aquachurch: Essential Leadership Arts for Piloting Your Church in Today's Fluid Culture* (Loveland, Colo.: Group, 1999), 24.

7. Ibid.

8. Zygmunt Bauman, *Liquid Modernity* (Cambridge, UK; Malden, Mass.: Polity Press, 2000).

9. Ibid., 3–4.

10. Ibid., 25, 35, 57, 63.

11. Ibid., 57.

12. Ibid., 5, 7, 13, 29, 31.

13. In the UK there is a growing movement toward youth congregations. Some are attached to existing churches, some are church plants, and some have grown from incarnational mission.

14. Bauman, *Liquid Modernity,* 10.

Notes to Chapter 2

1. For a more thorough periodization, see David Bosch, *Transforming Mission: Paradigm Shifts in Theology of Mission,* American Society of Mission Series 16 (Maryknoll, N.Y.: Orbis, 1991).

2. Anthony Giddens, *Modernity and Self-Identity: Self and Society in the Late Modern Age* (Cambridge, UK; Malden, Mass.: Polity Press; Stanford, Calif.: Stanford University Press, 1991), 5.

3. Ibid.

4. Ibid.

5. Zygmunt Bauman, *Liquid Modernity* (Cambridge, UK; Malden, Mass.: Polity Press, 2000), 33.

6. Ibid., 34ff.
7. Ulrich Beck, quoted in Bauman, *Liquid Modernity*, 37.
8. Bauman, *Liquid Modernity*, 37.
9. Ibid., 200.
10. Ibid., 182.
11. This idea was suggested to me by Kester Brewin.
12. P. Scannell, "For Anyone as Someone Structures," *Media Culture and Society* 22, no. 1 (January 2000): 5–24; See 5–6.

Notes to Chapter 3

1. Timothy Bradshaw, *The Olive Branch: An Evangelical Anglican Doctrine of the Church* (Carlisle: Paternoster for Latimer House, 1992), 241.
2. Ibid., 6.
3. J. D. G. Dunn, *The Theology of Paul the Apostle* (Edinburgh: T&T Clark; Grand Rapids, Mich.: Eerdmans, 1998), 390.
4. G. E. Ladd, *A Theology of the New Testament* (London: Lutterworth, 1974), 482.
5. C. K. Barrett, *The First Epistle to the Corinthians* (London: A. C. Black; New York: Harper & Row, 1968), 72.
6. Dunn, *The Theology of Paul the Apostle*, 397.
7. Ibid., 397–98.
8. Ibid., 398.
9. Ibid., 400.
10. Ibid., 401.
11. Ibid., 548.
12. Ibid., 551; see also F. F. Bruce, *1 and 2 Corinthians*, The New Century Bible Commentary (Grand Rapids, Mich.: Eerdmans, 1971), 120; Hans Küng, *The Church* (London: Search Press, 1968), 228.
13. Dunn, *The Theology of Paul the Apostle*, 548.
14. Ibid., 551.
15. Ibid., 554.
16. Ibid.
17. Ibid., 559.
18. Barrett, *First Epistle to the Corinthians*, 288.

Notes to Chapter 4

1. Zygmunt Bauman, *Liquid Modernity* (Cambridge, UK; Malden, Mass.: Polity Press, 2000), 2.

2. Ibid.
3. Ibid.
4. Manuel Castells, *The Rise of the Network Society* (2d ed.; Oxford: Blackwell, 2000), 164.
5. David Lyon, *Jesus in Disneyland: Religion in Postmodern Times* (Cambridge, UK; Malden, Mass.: Polity Press, 2000), 38.
6. Castells, *Rise of the Network Society,* 500.
7. Ibid., 443.
8. Ibid.
9. Ibid., 444.
10. Ibid., 442.
11. Ibid.

Notes to Chapter 5

1. See John D. Zizioulas, *Being as Communion: Studies in Personhood and the Church* (Crestwood, N.Y.: St. Vladimir's Seminary Press, 1985); Colin E. Gunton, *The Promise of Trinitarian Theology* (2d ed.; Edinburgh: T&T Clark, 1997); Miroslav Volf, *After Our Likeness: The Church as the Image of the Trinity* (Grand Rapids, Mich.: Eerdmans, 1998); James B. Torrance, *Worship and the Triune God of Grace* (Carlisle: Paternoster; Downers Grove, Ill.: InterVarsity Press, 1996); David S. Cunningham, *These Three Are One: The Practice of Trinitarian Theology,* Challenges in Contemporary Theology (Oxford: Blackwell, 1998); Paul S. Fiddes, *Participating in God: A Pastoral Doctrine of the Trinity* (London: Darton, Longman & Todd, 2000).
2. Gunton, *The Promise of Trinitarian Theology,* 5.
3. Ibid., 6.
4. Torrance, *Worship and the Triune God of Grace,* 21.
5. Athanasius Incarnation of the Word 54.3, *Athanasius: Selected Works and Letters,* ed. Archibald Robertson, in *Nicene and Post-Nicene Fathers,* second series, vol. 4, ed. Philip Schaff and Henry Wace (Peabody, Mass.: Hendrickson, 1995).
6. Torrance, *The Triune God of Grace,* 21.
7. Ibid.
8. Gunton, *The Promise of Trinitarian Theology,* 6.
9. Cunningham, *These Three Are One,* 8.
10. Zizioulas, *Being as Communion,* 17.
11. Ibid.
12. Ibid., 112.

13. Cunningham, *These Three Are One*, 8; Gunton, *The Promise of Trinitarian Theology*, 6.
14. Cunningham, *These Three Are One*, 25.
15. Robert W. Jenson, quoted in Cunningham, *These Three Are One*, 26.
16. Jürgen Moltmann, *The Crucified God* (London: SCM Press, 1974).
17. Moltmann, quoted in Cunningham, *These Three Are One*, 30.
18. Fiddes, *Participating in God*, 36.
19. Ibid., 34.
20. Ibid., 38.
21. Ibid.
22. Ibid., 72.
23. Ibid.
24. Ibid., 75.
25. Torrance, *Worship and the Triune God of Grace*, 20.
26. Gunton, *The Promise of Trinitarian Theology*, 81.
27. Ibid.
28. Ibid., 82.
29. Cunningham, *These Three Are One*, 8.

Notes to Chapter 6

1. Stephen Fry, quoting G. K. Chesterton, on the BBC television show *Room 101*.
2. See Grace Davie, *Religion in Britain Since 1945: Believing Without Belonging*, Making Contemporary Britain (Oxford: Blackwell, 1994); David Lyon, *Jesus in Disneyland: Religion in Postmodern Times* (Cambridge, UK; Malden, Mass.: Polity Press, 2000).
3. Robert Wuthnow, *Loose Connections: Joining Together in America's Fragmented Communities* (Cambridge, Mass. Harvard University Press, 1998), 2.
4. Davie, *Religion in Britain Since 1945*.
5. Ibid., 2.
6. Wuthnow, *Loose Connections*, 6.
7. Ibid., 7.
8. Ibid.
9. Zygmunt Bauman, *Liquid Modernity* (Cambridge, UK; Malden, Mass.: Polity Press, 2000), 73.
10. Ibid.

11. Jean Baudrillard, *Selected Writings,* ed. and with introduction by Mark Poster (Cambridge, UK; Malden, Mass.: Polity Press; Stanford, Calif.: Stanford University Press, 1988), 22.

12. Mike Featherstone, *Consumer Culture and Postmodernism* (London: Sage, 1991), 13.

13. James B. Twitchell, *Adcult USA* (New York: Columbia University Press, 1996), 10.

14. Ibid., 11.

15. Ibid., 12.

16. James B. Twitchell, *Lead Us into Temptation: The Triumph of American Materialism* (New York: Columbia University Press, 1999), 57.

17. Pierre Bourdieu, *Distinction: A Social Critique of the Judgment of Taste,* trans. Richard Nice (London: Routledge, 1986).

18. Twitchell, *Lead Us into Temptation,* 57.

19. David Lyon, *Jesus in Disneyland: Religion in Postmodern Times* (Cambridge, UK; Malden, Mass.: Polity Press, 2000), 74.

20. Ibid.

21. Peter Berger, cited in Lyon, *Jesus in Disneyland,* 76.

22. Reginald Bibby, quoted in Lyon, *Jesus in Disneyland,* 76. See Roger Finke and Rodney Stark, *The Churching of America 1776–1990: Winners and Losers in Our Religious Economy* (New Brunswick, N.J.: Rutgers University Press, 1992) for an alternative view of the importance of ecumenism for market share in religion.

23. R. Laurence Moore, *Selling God: American Religion in the Market Place of Culture* (Oxford: Oxford University Press, 1994).

24. Ibid., 5–7.

25. Ibid., 6.

26. See Nathan O. Hatch, *The Democratization of American Christianity* (New Haven, Conn.: Yale University Press, 1989); Jon Butler, *Awash In a Sea of Faith: Christianizing the American People* (Cambridge, Mass.: Harvard University Press, 1990); Leonard I. Sweet, ed., *Communication and Change in American Religious History* (Grand Rapids, Mich.: Eerdmans, 1993); Finke and Stark, *The Churching of America 1776–1990;* and Harry S. Stout, *The Divine Dramatist: George Whitefield and the Rise of Modern Evangelicalism* (Grand Rapids, Mich.: Eerdmans, 1991).

27. Stephan Hunt, *Anyone for Alpha? Evangelism in a Post-Christian Era* (London: Darton, Longman & Todd, 2001), xi.

28. P. Simmonds, *Reaching the Unchurched: Some Lessons from Willow Creek* (Bramcott: Grove Books, 1992), 14.

NOTES TO CHAPTER 7

1. John Calvin, *Institutes of the Christian Religion*, ed. John T. McNeill, trans. Ford Lewis Battles, 2 vols., The Library of Christian Classics 20 and 21 (Philadelphia: Westminster, 1960), 2:1021–22, 4.1.7.

2. Ibid., 2:1023–25, 4.1.9–10.

3. Ibid., 2:1023–24, 4.1.9.

4. Ibid.

5. Eberhard Busch, *Karl Barth: His Life from Letters and Autobiographical Texts* (trans. John Bowden; London: SCM Press; Philadelphia: Fortress, 1976), 263.

6. Karl Barth, *Church Dogmatics 1/1*, ed. G. W. Bromiley and T. F. Torrance (2d ed.; Edinburgh: T&T Clark, 1975), 3.

7. Ibid., 11.

8. Ibid., 72.

9. Ibid.

10. Ibid., 88.

11. Ibid.

12. Ibid., 78.

13. Ibid., 81.

14. Ibid., 80–81.

15. Andrew Walker, *Telling the Story: Gospel Mission and Culture* (London: SPCK, 1996), 13.

16. Ibid., 13–14.

17. Ibid., 12–13.

18. Ibid., 13–14.

NOTES TO CHAPTER 8

1. Tony Walter, *All You Love Is Need* (London: SPCK, 1985), 4.

2. Ibid.

3. Ibid., 5.

4. See chapter 6.

5. Zygmunt Bauman, *Liquid Modernity* (Cambridge, UK; Malden, Mass.: Polity Press, 2000), 74.

6. Ibid.

7. Paul Heelas, *The New Age Movement: The Celebration of the Self and the Sacralization of Modernity* (Oxford: Blackwell, 1996), 18.

8. See James Davison Hunter, *Evangelicalism: The Coming Generation* (Chicago: University of Chicago Press, 1987); and Leslie J. Francis and William K. Kay, *Teenage Religion and Values* (Leominster: Gracewing, 1995).

NOTES TO CHAPTER 9

1. Jürgen Moltmann, *The Spirit of Life: A Universal Affirmation* (London: SCM Press, 1992), 2.

2. Ibid.

3. Ibid., x.

4. Ibid.

5. Jürgen Moltmann, *The Trinity and the Kingdom of God* (London: SCM Press, 1981).

6. Moltmann, *The Spirit of Life*, x.

7. Ibid., 18.

8. Abraham Kuyper, "Common Grace," pages 165–204 in *Abraham Kuyper: A Centennial Reader*, ed. James D. Bratt (Grand Rapids, Mich.: Eerdmans; Carlisle: Paternoster, 1998), 172.

9. Ibid.

10. Ibid., 166.

11. Ibid., 168.

12. Ibid., 173.

13. Ibid., 174.

14. Ibid., 176.

15. Ibid., 174.

16. Ibid.

17. Jonathan Edwards, *The Religious Affections* (Edinburgh: Banner of Truth Trust, 1961), 25.

18. Ibid., 27.

19. Ibid., 50.

20. Ibid., 121.

21. Ibid., 122.

22. Ibid., 59.

23. Ibid., 69.

24. Ibid., 126.

25. Ibid., 85.

26. Ibid., 120ff.

NOTES TO CHAPTER 10

1. Zygmunt Bauman, *Liquid Modernity* (Cambridge, UK; Malden, Mass.: Polity Press, 2000), 77.

2. Daniel Miller, *A Theory of Shopping* (Cambridge, UK: Polity Press; repr., Ithaca, N.Y.: Cornell University Press, 1998), 18.

3. Eamon Duffy, *The Stripping of the Altars: Traditional Religion in England 1400–1580* (New Haven, Conn.: Yale University Press, 1992), 93.

4. Ibid., 97.

BIBLIOGRAPHY

Athanasisus. "The Incarnation of the Word." Pages 36–67 in *Athanasius: Selected Works and Letters*. Edited by Archibald Robertson. *Nicene and Post-Nicene Fathers*, second series, vol. 4. Edited by Philip Schaff and Henry Wace. Peabody, Mass.: Hendrickson, 1995.

Barrett, C. K. *The First Epistle to the Corinthians*. London: A & C Black; New York; Harper & Row, 1968.

Barth, Karl. *Church Dogmatics 1/1*. Edited by G. W. Bromiley and T. F. Torrance. 2d ed. Edinburgh: T&T Clark, 1975.

Baudrillard, Jean. *Selected Writings*. Edited and with introduction by Mark Poster. Cambridge, UK; Malden, Mass.: Polity Press; Stanford, Calif.: Stanford University Press, 1988.

Bauman, Zygmunt. *Liquid Modernity*. Cambridge, UK; Malden, Mass.: Polity Press, 2000.

Beck, Ulrich. *Risk Society: Toward a New Modernity*. Translated by Mark Ritter. London: Sage, 1992.

Bosch, David. *Transforming Mission: Paradigm Shifts in Theology of Mission*. American Society of Mission Series 16. Maryknoll, N.Y.: Orbis, 1991.

Bourdieu, Pierre. *Distinction: A Social Critique of the Judgment of Taste*. Translated by Richard Nice. London: Routledge, 1986.

Braaten, Carl E., and Robert W. Jenson, eds. *Christian Dogmatics*. 2 vols. Philadelphia: Fortress, 1984.

Bradshaw, Timothy. *The Olive Branch: An Evangelical Anglican Doctrine of the Church*. Carlisle: Paternoster for Latimer House, 1992.

Bratt, James D., ed. *Abraham Kuyper: A Centennial Reader*. Grand Rapids, Mich.: Eerdmans; Carlisle: Paternoster, 1998.

Bromiley, G. W. *Theological Dictionary of the New Testament*. Edited by Gerhard Kittel and Gerhard Friedrich. Abridged in one volume. Exeter: Paternoster; Grand Rapids, Mich.: Eerdmans, 1985.

Bruce, F. F. *1 and 2 Corinthians*. The New Century Bible Commentary. Grand Rapids, Mich.: Eerdmans, 1971.

Busch, Eberhard. *Karl Barth: His Life from Letters and Autobiographical Texts*. Translated by John Bowden. London: SCM Press; Philadelphia: Fortress, 1976.

Butler, Jon. *Awash In a Sea of Faith: Christianizing the American People*. Cambridge, Mass.: Harvard University Press, 1990.

Calvin, John. *Institutes of the Christian Religion*. Edited by John T. McNeill. Translated by Ford Lewis Battles. 2 vols. The Library of Christian Classics 20 and 21. Philadelphia: Westminster, 1960.

Carpenter, Joel A. *Revive Us Again: The Reawakening of American Fundamentalism*. Oxford: Oxford University Press, 1997.

Castells, Manuel. *The Rise of the Network Society*. 2d ed. Oxford: Blackwell, 2000.

Cunningham, David S. *These Three Are One: The Practice of Trinitarian Theology*. Challenges in Contemporary Theology. Oxford: Blackwell, 1998.

Davie, Grace. *Religion in Britain Since 1945: Believing Without Belonging*. Making Contemporary Britain. Oxford: Blackwell, 1994.

Duffy, Eamon. *The Stripping of the Altars: Traditional Religion in England 1400–1580*. New Haven, Conn.: Yale University Press, 1992.

Dulles, Avery. *Models of the Church*. Dublin: Gill and Macmillan, 1976.

Dunn, J. D. G. *The Theology of Paul the Apostle*. Edinburgh: T&T Clark; Grand Rapids, Mich.: Eerdmans, 1998.

Edwards, Jonathan. *The Religious Affections*. Edinburgh: Banner of Truth Trust, 1961.

Featherstone, Mike. *Consumer Culture and Postmodernism*. London: Sage, 1991.

Ferguson, Everett. *The Church of Christ: A Biblical Ecclesiology for Today*. Grand Rapids, Mich.: Eerdmans, 1996.

Fiddes, Paul S. *Participating in God: A Pastoral Doctrine of the Trinity*. London: Darton, Longman & Todd, 2000.

Finke, Roger, and Rodney Stark. *The Churching of America 1776–1990: Winners and Losers in Our Religious Economy*. New Brunswick, N.J.: Rutgers University Press, 1992.

Francis, Leslie J., and William K. Kay. *Teenage Religion and Values*. Leominster: Gracewing, 1995.

Giddens, Anthony. *Modernity and Self-Identity: Self and Society in the Late Modern Age*. Cambridge: Polity Press; Stanford, Calif.: Stanford University Press, 1991.

Gunton, Colin E. *The Promise of Trinitarian Theology*. 2d ed. Edinburgh: T&T Clark, 1997.

Hatch, Nathan O. *The Democratization of American Christianity*. New Haven, Conn.: Yale University Press, 1989.

Heelas, Paul. *The New Age Movement: The Celebration of the Self and the Sacralization of Modernity*. Oxford: Blackwell, 1996.

Hefner, P. J. "Ninth Locus: The Church." Pages 183–241 in *Christian Dogmatics*. Edited by Carl E. Braaten and Robert W. Jenson. 2 vols. Philadelphia: Fortress, 1984.

Hunt, Stephan. *Anyone for Alpha? Evangelism in a Post-Christian Era*. London: Darton, Longman & Todd, 2001.

Hunter, James Davison. *Evangelicalism: The Coming Generation*. Chicago: University of Chicago Press, 1987.

Jenkins, Henry. *Textual Poachers, Television Fans, and Participatory Culture*. London: Routledge, 1992.

Johnson, Douglas L. *Contending for the Faith: A History of the Evangelical Movement in the Universities and Colleges*. Leicester: Inter-Varsity Press, 1979.

Kay, William K., and Leslie J. Francis. *Drift from the Churches: Attitude Toward Christianity During Childhood and Adolescence*. Cardiff: University of Wales Press, 1996.

Küng, Hans. *The Church*. London: Search Press, 1968.

Kuyper, Abraham. "Common Grace." Pages 165–204 in *Abraham Kuyper: A Centennial Reader*. Edited by James D. Bratt. Grand Rapids, Mich.: Eerdmans; Carlisle: Paternoster, 1998.

Ladd, G. E. *A Theology of the New Testament*. London: Lutterworth, 1974.

Lyon, David. *Jesus in Disneyland: Religion in Postmodern Times*. Cambridge, UK; Malden, Mass.: Polity Press, 2000.

Miller, Daniel. *A Theory of Shopping*. Cambridge, UK: Polity Press, 1996. Repr., Ithaca, N.Y.: Cornell University Press, 1998.

Moltmann, Jürgen. *The Crucified God*. London: SCM Press, 1974.

———. *God in Creation: An Ecological Doctrine of Creation*. London: SCM Press, 1985.

———. *The Spirit of Life: A Universal Affirmation*. London: SCM Press, 1992.

————. *The Trinity and the Kingdom of God*. London: SCM Press, 1981.

Moore, R. Laurence. *Selling God: American Religion in the Market Place of Culture*. Oxford: Oxford University Press, 1994.

Pahl, Jon. *Youth Ministry in Modern America 1930—Present*. Peabody, Mass.: Hendrickson, 2000.

Rayburn, J., III. *Dance, Children, Dance*. Wheaton, Ill.: Tyndale House Publishers, 1984.

Scannell, P. "For Anyone as Someone Structures." *Media Culture and Society* 22, no. 1 (January 2000): 5–24.

Simmonds, P. *Reaching the Unchurched: Some Lessons from Willow Creek*. Bramcott: Grove Books, 1992.

Sweet, Leonard I. *Aquachurch: Essential Leadership Arts for Piloting Your Church in Today's Fluid Culture*. Loveland, Colo.: Group, 1999.

Torrance, James B. *Worship and the Triune God of Grace*. Carlisle: Paternoster; Downers Grove, Ill.: InterVarsity Press, 1996.

Twitchell, James B. *Adcult USA*. New York: Columbia University Press, 1995.

————. *Lead Us into Temptation: The Triumph of American Materialism*. New York: Columbia University Press, 1999.

Volf, Miroslav. *After Our Likeness: The Church as the Image of the Trinity*. Grand Rapids, Mich.: Eerdmans, 1998.

Walker, Andrew. *Telling the Story: Gospel Mission and Culture*. London: SPCK, 1996.

Walter, Tony. *All You Love Is Need*. London: SPCK, 1985.

Ward, Pete. *God at the Mall*. Peabody, Mass.: Hendrickson, 2000. Rev. and adapted from *Youthwork and the Mission of God: Frameworks for Relational Ministry*. London: SPCK, 1997.

Wuthrow, Robert. *Loose Connections: Joining Together in America's Fragmented Communities*. Cambridge, Mass.: Harvard University Press, 1998.

Zizioulas, John D. *Being as Communion: Studies in Personhood and the Church*. Crestwood, N.Y.: St. Vladimir's Seminary Press, 1985.

17484133R00066

Printed in Great Britain
by Amazon